Mark Antony & Cleopatra

By William Shakespeare

Edited by Julien Coallier

Copyright Julien Coallier 2012
All Rights Reserved.

Scenes

Act I – 9

Scene 1: A room in Cleopatra's palace. (Alexandria)

Scene 2: The same general location. Another room.

Scene 3: The same general location. Another room.

Scene 4: Octavius Caesar's house. (Rome)

Scene 5: Cleopatra's palace. (Alexandria)

Act II – 35

Scene 1: Messina. Pompey's house.

Scene 2: Rome. The house of Lepidus:

Scene 3: The same general location. Octavius Caesar's house.

Scene 4: The same general location. A street.

Scene 5: Alexandria. Cleopatra's palace.

Scene 6: Near Misenum.

Scene 7: On board Pompey's galley, off Misenum.

Act III – 73

Scene 1: A plain in Syria.

Scene 2: Rome. An ante-chamber in Octavius Caesar's house.

Scene 3: Cleopatra's palace. (Alexandria)

Scene 4: Athens. A room in Mark Anthony's house.

Scene 5: The same general location. Another room.

Scene 6: Rome. Octavius Caesar's house.

Scene 7: Near Actium. Mark Anthony's camp.

Scene 8: A plain near Actium.

Scene 9: Another part of the plain.

Scene 10: Another part of the plain.

Scene 11: Alexandria. Cleopatra's palace.

Scene 12: Egypt. Octavius Caesar's camp.

Scene 13: Cleopatra's palace. (Alexandria)

Act IV – 113

Scene 1: Before Alexandria. Octavius Caesar's camp.

Scene 2: Alexandria. Cleopatra's palace.

Scene 3: The same general location. Before the palace.

Scene 4: The same general location. A room in the palace.

Scene 5: Alexandria. Mark Anthony's camp.

Scene 6: Alexandria. Octavius Caesar's camp.

Scene 7: Field of battle between the camps.

Scene 8: Under the walls of Alexandria.

Scene 9: Octavius Caesar's camp.

Scene 10: Between the two camps.

Scene 11: Another part of the same general location.

Scene 12: Another part of the same general location.

Scene 13: Cleopatra's palace. (Alexandria)

Scene 14: Another room. (Alexandria)

Scene 15: A monument. (Alexandria)

Act V – 149

Scene 1: Alexandria. Octavius Caesar's camp.

Scene 2: Alexandria. A room in the monument.

Characters

Agrippa (Friend to Caesar)

Alexas (Attendant on Cleopatra)

All

Mark Anthony (Marcus Antonius)

Attendant

Attendants

Canidius (Lieutenant-general to Mark Anthony)

Captain

Charmain (Attendant on Cleopatra)

Cleopatra (Queen of Egypt)

Jester

Demetrius Friend to Mark Anthony)

Dercetas (Friend to Mark Anthony)

Diomedes, (Attendant on Cleopatra)

Dolabella (Friend to Caesar)

Domitius Enobarus (Friend to Mark Anthony)

Egyptian

Eros (Friend to Mark Anthony)

Euphronius (An ambassador from Mark Anthony to Caesar)

First Attendant

First Guard

First Officer

First Servant

First Soldier

Fourth Soldier

Gallus (Friend to Caesar)

Guard

Iras (Attendant on Cleopatra)

Lepidus (Marcus Antonius Lepidus)

Mardian a eunuch, attendant on Cleopatra)

Mecaenas (Friend to Caesar)

Menas (Friend to Caesar)

Menecrates, (Friend to Pompey)

Messenger

Octavia (Sister to Caesar and wife to Mark Anthony)

Octavius (Octavius Caesar)

Philo (Friend to Mark Anthony)

Pompey (Sextus Pompeius)

Proculeius (Friend to Caesar)

Scarus (Friend to Mark Anthony)

Second Attendant

Second Guard

Second Messenger

Second Officer

Second Servant

Second Soldier

Seleucus (Attendant on Cleopatra)

Silius (An officer in Ventidius's army)

Soldier

Soothsayer

Taurus (Lieutenant-general to Caesar)

Third Guard

Third Officer

Third Soldier

Thyreus (Friend to Caesar)

Varrius (Friend to Pompey)

Ventidius (Friend to Mark Anthony)

Act I, Scene 1

A room in Cleopatra palace. Alexandria.

(Demetrius and Philo enter)

Philo: Nay, but this doubting of our general's overflows the measure of his goodly eyes that over the files and musters of the war have glowed like plated Mars.

Now bend, now turn, the office and devotion of their view upon a tawny front.

His captain's heart, which in the scuffles of great fights hath burst the buckles on his breast; reforms all temper and is become the bellows and the fan to cool a gipsy's lust.

(Flourishing are provided as Mark Anthony, Cleopatra, her Ladies,)

the Entourage, with Eunuchs fanning her enter)

Look, where they come.

Take but good note, and you shall see in him.

The triple pillar of the world transformed into a strumpet's fool: behold and see.

Cleopatra: If it be love indeed, tell me how much.

Mark Anthony: There's beggary in the love that can be reckoned.

Cleopatra: I'll set a bourn how far to be beloved.

Mark Anthony: Then must thou needs find out new heaven, new earth.

(Enter an Attendant)

Attendant: News my good lord, from Rome.

Mark Anthony: Greates me as the sun.

Cleopatra: Nay, hear them,

Mark Anthony: Fulvia perchance is angry, or who knows.
If the scarce-bearded Caesar have not sent his powerful mandate to you, Do this, or this.
Take in that kingdom, and enfranchise that; perform it or else we damn thee.

Mark Anthony: How, my love!

Cleopatra: Perchance! Nay, and most like you must not stay here longer, your dismission is come from Caesar; therefore hear it.

Mark Anthony:
Where's Fulvia's process? Caesar's I would say? both?
Call in the messengers. As I am Egypt's queen.
Thou blushest Mark Anthony, and that blood of thine is Caesar's homage.
Else so thy cheek pays shame when shrill-tongued Fulvia scolds the messengers!

Mark Anthony: Let Rome in Tiber melt, and the wide arch of the ranged empire fall! For here is my space.
Kingdoms are clay, our dungy earth alike feeds beast as man.
The nobleness of life is to do thus; when such a mutual pair

(Embracing)

And such a twain can do it, in which I bind on pain of punishment the world to meet.
We stand up peerless.

Cleopatra: Excellent falsehood!

Why did he marry Fulvia, and not love her?

I'll seem the fool I am not, Mark Anthony, will be himself.

Mark Anthony: But I am stirred by Cleopatra now.

For the love of Love and her soft hours, let's not confound the time with conference harsh.

There's not a minute of our lives should stretch without some pleasure now.

What sport tonight?

Cleopatra: Hear the ambassadors.

Mark Anthony: Fie, wrangling queen!

Whom everything becomes, to chide, to laugh, to weep, whose every passion fully strives to make itself, in thee, fair and admired!

No messenger, but thine, and all alone to-night we'll wander through the streets and note the qualities of people.

Come, my queen, last night you did desire it: speak not to us.

(Exit Mark Anthony and Cleopatra with their entourage)

Demetrius: Is Caesar with Antonius prized so slight?

Philo: Sir, sometimes when he is not Mark Anthony, he comes too short of that great property which still should go with Mark Anthony.

Demetrius: I am full sorry that he approves the common liar who thus speaks of him at Rome.

But I will hope of better deeds to-morrow, rest you happy!

(Exit)

Act I, Scene 2

The same general location. Another room.

(Charmain, Iras, Alexas, and a Soothsayer enter)

Charmain: Lord Alexas, sweet Alexas, most anything Alexas, almost most absolute Alexas.

Where's the soothsayer that you praised so to the queen?

Oh, that I knew this husband, which, you say must charge his horns with garlands!

Alexas: Soothsayer!

Soothsayer: Your will?

Charmain: Is this the man? Is it you, sir, that know things?

Soothsayer: In nature's infinite book of secrecy; a little I can read.

Alexas: Show him your hand.

(Domitius Enobarus enters)

Domitius Enobarus: Bring in the banquet quickly, wine enough for Cleopatra's health to drink.

Charmain: Good sir, give me good fortune.

Soothsayer: I make not, but foresee.

Charmain: Pray, then, foresee me one.

Soothsayer: You shall be yet far fairer than you are.

Charmain: He means in flesh.

Iras: No, you shall paint when you are old.

Charmain: Wrinkles forbid!

Alexas: Vex not his prescience; be attentive.

Charmain: Hush!

Soothsayer: You shall be more beloving than beloved.

Charmain: I had rather heat my liver with drinking.

Alexas: Nay, hear him.

Charmain: Good now, some excellent fortune!
Let me be married to three kings in a forenoon, and widow them all.
Let me have a child at fifty, to whom Herod of Jewry may do homage.
Find me to marry me with Octavius Caesar, and companion me with my mistress.

Soothsayer: You shall outlive the lady whom you serve.

Charmain: Oh excellent! I love long life better than figs.

Soothsayer: You have seen and proved a fairer former fortune than that which is to approach.

Charmain: Then belike my children shall have no names.
Prithee, how many boys and wenches must I have?

Soothsayer: If every of your wishes had a womb and fertile every wish, a million.

Charmain: Out, fool! I forgive thee for a witch.

Alexas: You think none but your sheets are privy to your wishes.

Charmain: Nay, come, tell Iras hers.

Alexas: We'll know all our fortunes.

Domitius Enobarus: Mine, and most of our fortunes, to-night, shall
Be drunk to bed.

Iras: There's a palm presages chastity if nothing else.

Charmain: Even as the overflowing Nilus presageth famine.

Iras: Go, you wild bedfellow, you cannot soothsay.

Charmain: Nay, if an oily palm be not a fruitful prognostication, I cannot scratch mine ear.

Prithee, tell her but a worky-day fortune.

Soothsayer: Your fortunes are alike.

Iras: But how, but how? Give me particulars.

Soothsayer: I have said.

Iras: Am I not an inch of fortune better than she?

Charmain: Well, if you were but an inch of fortune better than I, where would you choose it?

Iras: Not in my husband's nose.

Charmain: Our worser thoughts heavens mend! Alexas come, his fortune, his fortune!

Oh, let him marry a woman that cannot go.

Sweet Isis, I beseech thee! and let her die too and give him a worse! And let worst follow worse, till the worst of all follow him laughing to his grave; fifty-fold a cuckold!

Good Isis, hear me this prayer, though thou deny me a matter of more weight.

Good Isis, I beseech thee!

Iras: Amen. Dear goddess, hear that prayer of the people!

For, as it is a heartbreaking to see a handsome man loose-wived; so it is a deadly sorrow to behold a foul knave uncuckolded.

Therefore, dear Isis, keep decorum and fortune him accordingly!

Charmain: Amen.

Alexas: Lord now, if it lay in their hands to make me a cuckold they would make themselves whores, but they would do it!

Domitius Enobarus: Hush! Here comes Mark Anthony.

Charmain: Not he, the queen.

(Cleopatra enters)

Cleopatra: Saw you my lord?

Domitius Enobarus: No, lady.

Cleopatra: Was he not here?

Charmain: No, madam.

Cleopatra: He was disposed to mirth but on the sudden, a Roman thought hath struck him.

Enobarbus!

Domitius Enobarus: Madam?

Cleopatra: Seek him, and bring him hither.

Where's Alexas?

Alexas: Here at your service, my lord approaches.

Cleopatra: We will not look upon him.

Go with us.

(Exit)

(Mark Anthony with a Messenger and Attendants enter)

Messenger: Fulvia thy wife first came into the field.

Mark Anthony: Against my brother Lucius?

Messenger: Ay, but soon that war had end, and the time's state made friends of them; joining their force against Caesar, whose better issue in the war from Italy, drave them upon the first encounter.

Mark Anthony: Well, what worst?

Messenger: The nature of bad news infects the teller.

Mark Anthony: When it concerns the fool or coward on things that are past are done with me, it is thus.

Who tells me true, though in his tale lie death, I hear him as he flattered.

Messenger: Labienus, this is stiff news; hath with his Parthian force extended Asia from Euphrates.

His conquering banner shook from Syria to Lydia, and to Ionia; all the while

Mark Anthony: Speak to me home, mince not the general tongue. I name Cleopatra, as she is called in Rome, rail thou in Fulvia's phrase; and taunt my faults with such full licence as both truth and malice have power to utter.

Oh, then we bring forth weeds when our quick minds lie still; and our ills told us is as our earing.

Fare thee well awhile.

Messenger: At your noble pleasure.

Mark Anthony: Mark Anthony, thou wouldst say

Messenger: Oh, my lord!

(Exit)

Mark Anthony: From Sicyon, oh, the news! Speak there!

First Attendant: The man from Sicyon.

Is there such an one?

Second Attendant: He stays upon your will.

Mark Anthony: Let him appear.

These strong Egyptian fetters I must break or lose myself in dotage.

(Enter another Messenger)

What are you?

Second Messenger: Fulvia thy wife is dead.

Mark Anthony: Where died she?

Second Messenger: In Sicyon:

Her length of sickness, with what else more serious, importeth thee to know what this bears.

(Gives a letter)

Mark Anthony: Forbear me.

(Exit Second Messenger)

There's a great spirit gone! Thus did I desire it.

What our contempt doth often hurl from us, we wish it ours again, the present pleasure.

By revolution lowering does the opposite of itself become; she's good, the hand could pluck her back that shoved her on being gone. I must from this enchanting queen break off ten thousand harms my idleness doth hatch, more than the ills I know.

How now! Enobarbus!

(Re-enter Domitius Enobarbus)

Domitius Enobarus: What's your pleasure, sir?

Mark Anthony: I must with haste from hence.

Domitius Enobarus: Why then? We kill all our women, we see how mortal an unkindness is to them if they suffer our departure; death's the word.

Mark Anthony: I must be gone.

Domitius Enobarus: Under a compelling occasion, let women die. It were pity to cast them away for nothing, though between them and a great cause, they should be esteemed nothing.
Cleopatra, catching but the least noise of this, dies instantly, I have seen her die twenty times upon far poorer moment; I do think there is mettle in death which commits some loving act upon her, she hath such a celerity in dying.

Mark Anthony: She is cunning past man's thought.

(Exit Alexas)

Domitius Enobarus: Alack sir, no her passions are made of nothing but the finest part of pure love.
We cannot call her winds and waters sighs and tears, they are greater storms and tempests than almanacs can report.
This cannot be cunning in her if it be, she makes a shower of rain as well as love.

Mark Anthony: Would I? I had never seen her.

Domitius Enobarus: Oh sir, you had then left unseen a wonderful piece of work which would have discredited your travel, not to have been blessed with all.

Mark Anthony: Fulvia is dead.

Domitius Enobarus: Sir?

Mark Anthony: Fulvia is dead.

Domitius Enobarus: Fulvia!

Mark Anthony: Dead.

Domitius Enobarus: Why sir, give the gods a thankful sacrifice when it pleaseth their deities to take the wife of a man from him; it shows to man the tailors of the earth; comforting therein that.
When old robes are worn out, there are members to make new; if there were no more women but Fulvia then had you indeed a cut and the case to be lamented,
This grief is crowned with consolation, your old smock brings forth a new petticoat and indeed the tears live in an onion that should water this sorrow.

Mark Anthony: The business she hath broached in the state cannot endure my absence.

Domitius Enobarus: And the business you have broached here cannot be without you, especially that of Cleopatra's, which wholly depends on your abode.

Mark Anthony: No more light answers, let our officers have notice what we purpose.
I shall break the cause of our expedience to the queen and get her leave to part; for not alone the death of Fulvia, with more urgent touches do strongly speak to us, but the letters too, of many our contriving friends in Rome.
Petition us at home, Sextus Pompeius hath given the dare to Caesar, and commands the empire of the sea.

Mark Anthony: Our slippery people, whose love is never linked to the deserver till his deserts are past, begin to throw Pompey the Great and all his dignities upon his son; whose high in name and power, is higher than both in blood and life.

Stands up, for the main soldier, whose quality going on the sides of the world may danger, much is breeding which, like the courser's hair, hath yet but life; and not a serpent's poison.

Say our pleasure, to such whose place is under us, requires our quick remove from hence.

Domitius Enobarus: I shall do it.

(Exit)

Act I, Scene 3

The same general location. Another room.

(Cleopatra, Charmain, Iras, and Alexas enter)

Cleopatra: Where is he?

Charmain: I did not see him since.

Cleopatra: See where he is, who's with him, what he does. I did not send you if you find him sad; say I am dancing if in mirth. Report that I am sudden sick, quickly, and return.

(Exit Alexas)

Charmain: Madam, methinks, if you did love him dearly you do not hold the method to enforce the like from him.

Cleopatra: What should I do, I do not?

Charmain: In each thing give him way, cross him nothing.

Cleopatra: Thou teachest like a fool; the way to lose him.

Charmain: Tempt him not so too far, I wish, forbear, in time we hate that which we often fear; but here comes Mark Anthony.

(Mark Anthony enters)

Cleopatra: I am sick and sullen.

Mark Anthony: I am sorry to give breathing to my purpose.

Cleopatra: Help me away dear Charmain, I shall fall. It cannot be thus long, the sides of nature will not sustain it.

Mark Anthony: Now, my dearest queen.

Cleopatra: Pray you, stand further from me.

Mark Anthony: What's the matter?

Cleopatra: I know, by that same eye, there's some good news.

What says the married woman? You may go, would she had never given you leave to come!

Let her not say it is I that keep you here, I have no power upon you; hers you are.

Mark Anthony: The gods best know.

Cleopatra: Oh, never was there queen so mightily betrayed! Yet at the first I saw the treasons planted.

Mark Anthony: Cleopatra.

Cleopatra: Why should I think you can be mine and true in thought, you in swearing shake the throned gods who have been false to Fulvia?

Riotous madness to be entangled with those mouth-made vows, which break themselves in swearing!

Mark Anthony: Most sweet queen.

Cleopatra: Nay, pray you, seek no colour for your going, but bid farewell, and go.

When you sued staying, then was the time for words, no going then.

Cleopatra: Eternity was in our lips and eyes, bliss in our brows' bent, none our parts so poor, but was a race of heaven; they are so still; or thou, the greatest soldier of the world, art turned the greatest liar.

Mark Anthony: How now, lady!

Cleopatra: I would I had thy inches; thou shouldst know there were a heart in Egypt.

Mark Anthony: Hear me, queen.

The strong necessity of time commands our services awhile, but my full heart remains in use with you.

Our Italy shines over with civil swords.

Sextus Pompeius makes his approaches to the port of Rome; equality of two domestic powers breed scrupulous faction.

The hated grown to strength are newly grown to love, the condemned Pompey, rich in his father's honour, creeps apace into the hearts of such as have not thrived upon the present state; whose numbers threaten and quietness grown sick of rest, would purge by any desperate change.

My more particular, and that which most with you should safe my going, is Fulvia's death.

Cleopatra: Though age from folly could not give me freedom it does from childishness. Can Fulvia die?

Mark Anthony: She's dead, my queen.

Look here, and at thy sovereign leisure read the garboils.

She awaked at the last, best see when and where she died.

Cleopatra: Oh most false love!

Where be the sacred vials thou shouldst fill with sorrowful water?

Cleopatra: Now I see, I see, in Fulvia's death, how mine received shall be.

Mark Anthony: Quarrel no more, but be prepared to know the purposes I bear; which are, or cease as you shall give the advice. By the fire that quickens Nilus' slime, I go from hence thy soldier, servant; making peace or war; as thou affect'st.

Cleopatra: Cut my lace, Charmain, come, but let it be.
I am quickly ill, and well so Mark Anthony loves.

Mark Anthony: My precious queen forbear, and give true evidence to his love, which stands an honourable trial.

Cleopatra: So Fulvia told me.
I prithee, turn aside and weep for her, then bid adieu to me and say the tears belong to Egypt.
Be good now, play one scene of excellent dissembling, and let it look life perfect honour.

Mark Anthony: You'll heat my blood: no more.

Cleopatra: You can do better yet; but this is meetly.

Mark Anthony: Now, by my sword.

Cleopatra: And target. Still he mends, but this is not the best.
Look, prithee Charmain, how this Herculean Roman does become the carriage of his chafe.

Mark Anthony: I'll leave you, lady.

Cleopatra: Courteous lord, one word.
Sir, you and I must part, but that's not it.
Sir, you and I have loved, but there's not it; that you know well.
Something it is I would, oh my oblivion is a very Mark Anthony, and I am all forgotten.

Mark Anthony: But that your royalty holds idleness your subject, I should take you for idleness itself.

Cleopatra: It is sweating labour to bear such idleness so near the heart as Cleopatra this, but sir, forgive me since my becomings kill me when they do not eye well to you.

Your honour calls you hence, therefore be deaf to my unpitied folly, and all the gods go with you!

Upon your sword sit laurel victory! And smooth success be strewed before your feet!

Mark Anthony: Let us go. Come our separation so abides, and flies; that thou residing here go'st yet with me, and I, hence fleeting, here remain with thee.

Away!

(Exit)

Act I, Scene 4

Octavius Caesar's house. (Rome)

(Octavius Caesar, reading a letter, Lepidus, and their entourage enter)

Octavius: You may see, Lepidus, and henceforth know,
It is not Caesar's natural vice to hate our great competitor from Alexandria
This is the news: he fishes, drinks, and wastes the lamps of night in revel, is not more man-like than Cleopatra; nor the queen of Ptolemy more womanly than, he hardly gave audience.
Vouchsafed to think he had partners, you shall find there a man who is the abstract of all faults that all men follow.

Lepidus: I must not think there are evils now to darken all his goodness, his faults in him seem as the spots of heaven; more fiery by night's blackness; hereditary rather than purchased,
What he cannot change than what he chooses.

Octavius: You are too indulgent.
Let us grant, it is not amiss to tumble on the bed of Ptolemy, to give a kingdom for a mirth to sit and keep the turn of tippling with a slave.
To reel the streets at noon, and stand the buffet with knives that smell of sweat
Say this becomes him, as his composure must be rare, rare indeed whom these things cannot blemish; yet must Mark Anthony no way excuse his soils when we do bear so great weight in his lightness.

If he filled his vacancy with his voluptuousness, full surfeits and the dryness of his bones, call on him forth, but to confound such time that drums him from his sport and speaks as loud as his own state and ours.

It is to be child as we rate boys, who, being mature in knowledge pawn their experience to their present pleasure and so rebel to judgment.

(Messenger enters)

Lepidus: Here's more news.

Messenger: Thy biddings have been done; and every hour most noble Caesar; shalt thou have report how it is abroad.

Pompey is strong at sea and it appears he is beloved of those that only have feared Caesar: to the ports.

The discontents repair, and men's reports give him much wronged.

Octavius: I should have known no less.

It hath been taught us from the primal state, which was wished until he were, and the ebb'd man, never loved till never worth love comes deared by being lacked.

This common body, like to a vagabond, flag upon the stream; goes to and back lackeying the varying tide, to rot itself with motion.

Messenger: Caesar, I bring thee word, Menecrates and Menas, famous pirates, make the sea serve them, which they ear and wound with keels of every kind.

Many hot inroads they make in Italy, the borders maritime lack blood to think on it, and flush youth revolt.

No vessel can peep forth, but it is as soon taken as seen, for Pompey's name strikes more than could his war resisted.

Octavius: Mark Anthony, leave thy lascivious wassails.

When thou once was the beaten from Modena, where thou slew'st Hirtius and Pansa, consuls at thy heel, did famine follow; whom thou fought'st against, though daintily brought up with patience more than savages could suffer.

Thou didst drink the stale of horses and the gilded puddle, which beasts would cough at thy palate, then did deign the roughest berry on the rudest hedge; yea, like the stag, when snow the pasture sheets, the barks of trees thou browsed'st on the Alps.

It is reported thou didst eat strange flesh which some did die to look on, and all this it wounds thine honour that I speak it now, was borne so like a soldier; that thy cheek so much as lanked not.

Lepidus: It is pity of him.

Octavius: Let his shames quickly, drive him to Rome.

It is time we twain did show ourselves in the field, and to that end assemble we immediate council.

Pompey thrives in our idleness.

Lepidus: To-morrow, Caesar, I shall be furnished to inform you rightly both what by sea and land I can be able to front this present time.

Octavius: Till which the encounter it is my business too.

Farewell.

Lepidus: Farewell, my lord.

What you shall know meantime, of stirs abroad, I shall beseech you, sir to let me be partaker.

Octavius: Doubt not, sir, I knew it for my bond.

(Exit)

Act I, Scene 5

Cleopatra's palace. (Alexandria)

(Enter Cleopatra, Charmain, Iras, and Mardian)

Cleopatra: Charmain!

Charmain: Madam?

Cleopatra: Ha, ha! Give me to drink mandragora.

Charmain: Why, madam?

Cleopatra: That I might sleep out this great gap of time
My Mark Anthony is away.

Charmain: You think of him too much.

Cleopatra: Oh, it is treason!

Charmain: Madam, I trust, not so.

Cleopatra: Thou you owe as much Mardian!

Mardian: What's your highness' pleasure?

Cleopatra: Not now to hear thee sing, I take no pleasure in aught as one owed much has.

It is well for thee that being unseminared, thy freer thoughts may not fly forth of Egypt.

Hast thou affections?

Mardian: Yes, gracious madam.

Cleopatra: Indeed!

Mardian: Not in deed, madam; for I can do nothing, but what indeed is honest to be done.

Yet have I fierce affections, and think what Venus did with Mars.

Cleopatra: O hCharmain,

Where think'st thou he is now? Stands he, or sits he?

Or does he walk? or is he on his horse?

Oh happy horse, to bear the weight of Mark Anthony!

Do bravely, horse! for wot'st thou whom thou movest?

The demi-Atlas of this earth, the arm and burgonet of men.

He's speaking now, or murmuring, where's my serpent of old Nile?

For so he calls me, now I feed myself with most delicious poison.

Think on me, that am with Phoebus' amorous pinches black and wrinkled deep in time?

Broad-fronted Caesar, when thou was it here above the ground, I was a morsel for a monarch; and great Pompey would stand and make his eyes grow in my brow, there would he anchor his aspect and die with looking on his life.

(Alexas enters under banner of Octavius Caesar)

Alexas: Sovereign of Egypt, hail!

Cleopatra: How much unlike art thou Mark Anthony!

Yet, coming from him, that great medicine hath with his tinct gilded thee.

How goes it with my brave Mark Anthony?

Alexas: Last thing he did, dear queen, He kissed the last of many doubled kisses upon this orient pearl.

His speech sticks in my heart.

Cleopatra: Mine ear must pluck it thence.

Alexas: Good friend, quoth I of he, Say the firm Roman to great Egypt sends

this treasure of an oyster, at Cleopatra's foot, to mend the petty present.

I will piece her opulent throne with kingdoms all the east, say thou shall call her mistress.

So he nodded, and soberly did mount an arm-gaunt steed, who neighed so high that what I would have spoke was beastly dumbed by him.

Cleopatra: What, was he sad or merry?

Alexas: Like to the time of the year between the extremes of hot and cold; he was nor sad nor merry.

Cleopatra: Of well-divided disposition! Note him.

Good Charmain it is the man but note him.

He was not sad for he would shine on those that make their looks by his, he was not merry which seemed to tell them his remembrance lay in Egypt with his joy; but between both Oh heavenly mingle! Best thou sad or merry the violence of either thee becomes, so does it no man else. Met'st thou my posts?

Alexas: Ay, madam, twenty several messengers:

Why do you send so thick?

Cleopatra: Who's born that day when I forget to send to Mark Anthony, shall die a beggar, based upon Ink and paper, Charmain, Welcomed my good Alexas did I, Charmain, ever love Caesar so?

Charmain: Oh that brave Caesar!

Cleopatra: Be choked with such another emphasis!

Say the brave Mark Anthony.

Charmain: The valiant Caesar!

Cleopatra: By Isis, I will give thee bloody teeth if thou with Caesar paragon again

my man of men.

Charmain: By your most gracious pardon, I sing but after you.

Cleopatra: My salad days when I was green in judgment.

Cold in blood to say as I said then! But come away, get me ink and paper.

He shall have every day a several greeting, or I'll unpeople Egypt.

(Exit)

Act II, Scene 1

Pompey's house. (Messina)

(Pompey, Menecrates, and Menas, enter in a warlike manner)

Pompey: If the great gods be just, they shall assist the deeds of justest men.

Menecrates: Know, worthy Pompey, that what they do delay, they not deny.

Pompey: Whiles we are suitors to their throne, decays the thing we sue for.

Menecrates: We, ignorant of ourselves, beg often our own harms, which the wise powers deny us for our good; so find we profit by losing of our prayers.

Pompey: I shall do well.

The people love me, and the sea is mine; my powers are crescent, and my auguring hope says it will come to the full.

Pompey: Mark Anthony in Egypt sits at dinner and will make no wars without doors.

Caesar gets money where he loses hearts.

Lepidus flatters both; of both is flattered but he neither loves nor either cares for him.

Menas: Caesar and Lepidus are in the field a mighty strength, they carry force.

Pompey: Where have you this? It is false.

Menas: From Silvius sir.

Pompey: He dreams, I know they are in Rome together looking for Mark Anthony, but all the charms of love salt Cleopatra; soften thy waned lip!

Let witchcraft join with beauty, lust with both!

Tie up the libertine in a field of feasts, keep his brain fuming.

Epicurean cooks sharpen with cloyless sauce, his appetite that sleep, and feeding may prorogue his honour even till a Lethe'd dulness!

(Enter Varrius)

How now, Varrius!

Varrius: This is most certain that I shall deliver Mark Anthony, such is expected at every hour in Rome, since he went from Egypt it is a space for further travel.

Pompey: I could have given less matter a better ear Menas, I did not think this amorous surfeiter would have donn'd his helm for such a petty war.

His soldiership is twice the other twain, but let us rear the higher our opinion, that our stirring can from the lap of Egypt's widow pluck the never-lust-wearied Mark Anthony.

Menas: I cannot hope Caesar and Mark Anthony shall well greet together, his wife that's dead did trespasses to Caesar.

His brother warred upon him, although I think not moved by Mark Anthony.

Pompey: I know not, Menas, how lesser enmities may give way to greater.

Were it not that we stand up against them all, were they pregnant, it should square between themselves; for they have entertained cause enough to draw their swords, but how the fear of us may cement their divisions and bind up the petty difference.

We yet not know, be it as our gods will have it! It only stands our lives upon to use our strongest hands.

Come, Menas.

(Exit)

Act II, Scene 2

The house of Lepidus. (Rome)

(Domitius Enobarus and Lepidus enter)

Lepidus: Good Enobarbus, it is a worthy deed and shall become you well, to entreat your captain, to soft and gentle speech.

Domitius Enobarus: I shall entreat him to answer like himself; if Caesar move him, let Mark Anthony look over Caesar's head and speak as loud as Mars.

By Jupiter, were I the wearer of Antonius' beard, I would not shave it to-day.

Lepidus: it is not a time for private stomaching.

Domitius Enobarus: Every time serves for the matter that is then born in it.

Lepidus: But small to greater matters must give way.

Domitius Enobarus: Not if the small come first.

Lepidus: Your speech is passion, but pray you, stir no embers up. Here comes the noble Mark Anthony.

(Mark Anthony and Ventidius enter)

Domitius Enobarus: And yonder, Caesar.

(Enter Octavius Caesar, Mecaenas, and Agrippa)

Mark Anthony: If we compose well here, to Parthia: Hark, Ventidius:

Octavius: I do not know Mecaenas, ask Agrippa.

Lepidus: Noble friends, that which combined us was most great, and let not a leaner action rend us what's amiss.

May it be gently heard when we debate our trivial difference aloud.

We do commit murder in healing wounds then the rather, noble partners, for I earnestly beseech, touch you the sourest points with sweetest terms, nor curstness grow to the matter.

Mark Anthony: it is spoken well, were we before our armies, and to fight I should do thus.

(Flourish)

Octavius: Welcome to Rome.

Mark Anthony: Thank you.

Octavius: Sit.

Mark Anthony: Sit, sir.

Octavius: Nay, then.

Mark Anthony: I learn you take things ill which are not so, or being concern you not.

Octavius: I must be laughed at, if or for nothing or a little; I should say myself offended, and with you Chiefly, if the world would be more laughed at; that I should once name you derogately when to sound your name it not concerned me.

Mark Anthony: My being in Egypt, Caesar, what was it to you?

Octavius: No more than my residing here at Rome might be to you in Egypt, yet if you there did practise on my state, your being in Egypt might be my question.

Mark Anthony: How intend you practised?

Octavius: You may be pleased to catch at mine intent

By what did here befal me, your wife and brother made wars upon me; and their contestation was theme for you, you were the word of war.

Mark Anthony: You do mistake your business, my brother never did urge me in his act, I did inquire it;
And have my learning from some true reports that drew their swords with you; did he not rather discredit my authority with yours, and make the wars alike against my stomach having alike your cause? Of this my letters before did satisfy you, if you'll patch a quarrel. As matter whole you have not to make it with, it must not be with this.

Octavius: You praise yourself by laying defects of judgment to me; but you patched up your excuses.

Mark Anthony: Not so, not so;
I know you could not lack, I am certain on it.
Very necessity of this thought, that I, your partner in the cause against which he fought could not with graceful eyes attend those wars which fronted mine own peace.
As for my wife, I would you had her spirit in such another.
The third of the world is yours, which with a snaffle you may pace easy, but not such a wife.

Domitius Enobarus: Would we had all such wives, that the men might go to wars with the women!

Mark Anthony: So much uncurbable, her garboils, Caesar made out of her impatience, which not wanted.

Shrewdness of policy too, I grieving grant, did you too much disquiet.

For that you must must say, I could not help it.

Octavius: I wrote to you when rioting in Alexandria, you did pocket up my letters; and with taunts did gibe my missive out of audience.

Mark Anthony: Sir he fell upon me here admitted, then three kings I had newly feasted, and did want ff what I was in the morning; but next day I told him of myself, which was as much as to have asked him pardon.

Let this fellow, be nothing of our strife; if we contend out of our question wipe him.

Octavius: You have broken the article of your oath, which you shall never have tongue to charge me with.

Lepidus: Soft, Caesar!

Mark Anthony: No Lepidus, let him speak the honour is sacred, which he talks on now, supposing that I lacked it; but on Caesar the article of my oath.

Octavius: To lend me arms and aid when I required them, the which you both denied.

Mark Anthony: Neglected, rather; and then when poisoned hours had bound me up from mine own knowledge.

As nearly as I may, I'll play the penitent to you, but mine honesty shall not make poor my greatness, nor my power work without it.

Truth is, that Fulvia, to have me out of Egypt, made wars here for which myself, the ignorant motive, do so far ask pardon as befits mine honour to stoop in such a case.

Lepidus: it is noble spoken.

Mecaenas: If it might please you, to enforce no further the griefs between ye; to forget them quite; we are to remember that the present need Speaks to atone you.

Lepidus: Worthily spoken,

Mecaenas: Domitius

Enobarus: Or, if you borrow one another's love for the instant, you may when you hear no more words of Pompey, return it again. You shall have time to wrangle in when you have nothing else to do.

Mark Anthony: Thou art a soldier only: speak no more.

Domitius Enobarus: That truth should be silent I had almost forgot.

Mark Anthony: You wrong this presence; therefore speak no more.

Domitius Enobarus: Go to, then; your considerate stone.

Octavius: I do not much dislike the matter, but the manner of his speech; for it cannot be
We shall remain in friendship, our conditions so differing in their acts.
Yet if I knew what hoop should hold us stanch, from edge to edge of the world I would pursue it.

Agrippa: Give me leave, Caesar,

Octavius: Speak, Agrippa.

Agrippa: Thou hast a sister by the mother's side,

Admired Octavia: great Mark Anthony is now a widower.

Octavius: Say not so, Agrippa.

If Cleopatra heard you, your reproof were well deserved of rashness.

Mark Anthony: I am not married, Caesar: let me hear agrippa further speak.

Agrippa: To hold you in perpetual amity, to make you brothers, and to knit your hearts
With an unslipping knot.

Take Mark Anthony, Octavia, to his wife; whose beauty claims no worse a husband than the best of men; whose virtue and whose general graces speak that which none else can utter.

By this marriage, all little jealousies which now seem great, and all great fears, which now import their dangers, would then be nothing.

Truths would be tales where now half tales be truths, her love to both would; each to other and all loves to both draw after her.

Pardon what I have spoke, for it is a studied, not a present thought by duty ruminated.

Mark Anthony: Will Caesar speak?

Octavius: Not till he hears how Mark Anthony is touched with what is spoke already.

Mark Anthony: What power is in Agrippa,
If I would say, Agrippa, be it so, to make this good?

Octavius: The power of Caesar, and his power unto Octavia.

Mark Anthony: May I never
To this good purpose, that so fairly shows, dream of impediment!

Let me have thy hand further this act of grace, and from this hour the heart of brothers govern in our loves and sway our great designs!

Octavius: There is my hand.

A sister I bequeath you, whom no brother did ever love so dearly. Let her live to join our kingdoms and our hearts, and never fly off our loves again!

Lepidus: Happily, amen!

Mark Anthony: I did not think to draw my sword against Pompey; for he hath laid strange courtesies and great of late upon me. I must thank him only, lest my remembrance suffer ill report at heel of that, defy him.

Lepidus: Time calls upon us, Pompey must presently be sought, or else he seeks out us.

Mark Anthony: Where lies he?

Octavius: About the mount Misenum.

Mark Anthony: What is his strength by land?

Octavius: Great and increasing, but by sea he is an absolute master.

Mark Anthony: So is the fame.

Would we had spoke together! Haste we for it yet here we put ourselves in arms, dispatch we the business we have talked of.

Octavius: With most gladness, and do invite you to my sister's view, Whither straight I'll lead you.

Mark Anthony: Let us, Lepidus, not lack your company.

Lepidus: Noble Mark Anthony, not sickness should detain me.

(Flourish. Exit Octavius Caesar, Mark Anthony and Lepidus)

Mecaenas: Welcome from Egypt, sir.

Domitius Enobarus: Half the heart of Caesar, worthy Mecaenas! My honourable friend, Agrippa!

Agrippa: Good Enobarbus!

Mecaenas: We have cause to be glad that matters are so well digested, you stayed well by it in Egypt.

Domitius Enobarus: Ay, sir; we did sleep day out of countenance and made the night light with drinking.

Mecaenas: Eight wild-boars roasted whole at a breakfast, and but twelve persons there is this true?

Domitius Enobarus: This was but as a fly by an eagle: we had much more

monstrous matter of feast, which worthily deserved noting.

Mecaenas: She's a most triumphant lady, if report be square to her.

Domitius Enobarus: When she first met Mark Anthony, she pursed up his heart, upon the river of Cydnus.

Agrippa: There she appeared indeed; or my reporter devised well for her.

Domitius Enobarus: I will tell you.

The barge she sat in, like a burnished throne burned on the water, the strife was beaten gold; purple the sails and so perfumed that the winds were love-sick with them, the oars were silver which to the tune of flutes kept stroke, and made the water which they beat to follow faster, as amorous of their strokes.

For her own person, it beggared all description, she did lie in her pavilion cloth-of-gold of tissue over-picturing that Venus, where we see the fancy outwork nature.

On each side her Stood pretty dimpled boys, like smiling Cupids, with divers-coloured fans, whose wind did seem to glow the delicate cheeks which they did cool, and what they undid did.

Agrippa: Oh, rare for Mark Anthony!

Domitius Enobarus: Her gentlewomen, like the Nereides,
So many mermaids, tended her in the eyes, and made their bends adornings.

At the helm a seeming mermaid steers the silken tackle swell with the touches of those flower-soft hands; that yarely frame the office. From the barge a strange invisible perfume hits the sense of the adjacent wharfs.

Domitius Enobarus: The city cast her people out upon her; and Mark Anthony, enthroned in the market-place, did sit alone;

whistling to the air which, but for vacancy, had gone to gaze on Cleopatra too, and made a gap in nature.

Agrippa: Rare Egyptian!

Domitius Enobarus: Upon her landing, Mark Anthony sent to her, invited her to supper: she replied, it should be better he became her guest; which she entreated our courteous Mark Anthony.

Mark Anthony whom never the word of 'No' woman heard speak, being barbered ten times over, goes to the feast, and for his ordinary pays his heart for what his eyes eat only.

Agrippa: Royal wench!

She made great Caesar lay his sword to bed, he ploughed her, and she cropped.

Domitius Enobarus: I saw her once hop forty paces through the public street, and having lost her breath she spoke and panted; that she did make defect perfection, and breathless power breathe forth.

Mecaenas: Now Mark Anthony must leave her utterly.

Domitius Enobarus: Never; he will not age, cannot wither her, nor custom stale her infinite variety.

Other women cloy the appetites they feed, but she makes hungry where most she satisfies; for vilest things become themselves in her, that the holy priests bless her when she is riggish.

Mecaenas: If beauty, wisdom, modesty, can settle the heart of Mark Anthony, Octavia is a blessed lottery to him.

Agrippa: Let us go, good Enobarbus, make yourself my guest whilst you abide here.

Domitius Enobarus: Humbly, sir, I thank you.

(Exit)

Act II, Scene 3

Octavius Caesar's house

(Mark Anthony, Octavius Caesar's, Octavia between them, and Attendants enter)

Mark Anthony: The world and my great office will sometimes divide me from your bosom.

Octavia: All which time before the gods my knee shall bow my prayers to them for you.

Mark Anthony: Good night, sir. My Octavia, read not my blemishes in the world's report.

I have not kept my square, but that to come shall all be done by the rule.

Good night, dear lady.

Good night, sir.

Octavius: Good night.

(Exit Octavius Caesar's and Octavia)

(Soothsayer enters)

Mark Anthony: Now, sirrah; you do wish yourself in Egypt?

Soothsayer: Would I had never come from thence, nor you Thither!

Mark Anthony: If you can, your reason?

Soothsayer: I see it in my motion, have it not in my tongue, but yet here is you to Egypt again.

Mark Anthony: Say to me, whose fortunes shall rise higher, Caesar's or mine?

Soothsayer: Caesar's.

Therefore, Oh Mark Anthony, stay not by his side, thy demon, that's thy spirit which keeps thee, is Noble.

Courageous high, unmatchable, where Caesar's is not, but near him, thy angel becomes a fear, as being overpowered; therefore make space enough between you.

Mark Anthony: Speak this no more.

Soothsayer: To none but thee, no more, but when to thee, if thou dost play with him at any game, thou art sure to lose; and of that natural luck, he beats thee against the odds thy lustre thickens, when he shines by.

I say again, thy spirit is all afraid to govern thee near him, but, he away, it is noble.

Mark Anthony: Get thee gone.

Say to Ventidius I would speak with him:

(Exit Soothsayer)

He shall to Parthia, be it art or hap, he hath spoken true.

The very dice obey him, and in our sports my better cunning faints under his chance.

If we draw lots, he speeds his cocks to win the battle still of mine, when it is all to nought; and his quails ever beat mine.

In hooped, at odds I will to enter Egypt, and though I make this marriage for my peace, it is the east my pleasure lies.

(Ventidius enters)

Oh, come, you must to Parthia, your commission's ready.

Follow me, and receive it.

(Exit)

Act II, Scene 4

A street. (The same)

(Lepidus, Mecaenas, and Agrippa enter)

Lepidus: Trouble yourselves no further, pray you, hasten tour generals after.

Agrippa: Sir, Mark Anthony will even but kiss Octavia, and we'll follow.

Lepidus: Till I shall see you in your soldier's dress, which will become you both, farewell.

Mecaenas: We shall, as I conceive the journey, be at the Mount before you, Lepidus.

Lepidus: Your way is shorter; my purposes do draw me much about. You'll win two days upon me.

Mecaenas: (with Agrippa) Sir, good success!

Lepidus: Farewell.

(Exit)

Act II, Scene 5

Alexandria. **Cleopatra's** palace.

(Cleopatra, Charmain, Iras, and Alexas enter)

Cleopatra: Give me some music; music, moody food of us that trade in love.

Attendants: The music, oh!

(Enter Mardian)

Cleopatra: Let it alone, let's to billiards come, Charmain.

Charmain: My arm is sore; best play with Mardian.

Cleopatra: As well a woman with an eunuch played, as with a woman.

Come, you'll play with me, sir?

Mardian: As well as I can, madam.

Cleopatra: And when good will is showed, though't come too short, the actor may plead pardon. I'll none now.

Cleopatra: Give me mine angle, we'll to the river there, my music playing far off, I will betray

tawny-finned fishes; my bended hook shall pierce their slimy jaws, and as I draw them up

I'll think them every one an Mark Anthony and say 'Ah, ha! you're caught.'

Charmain: It was merry when you wagered on your angling, when your diver did hang a salt-fish on his hook; which he with fervency drew up. 1070

Cleopatra: That time, Oh times! I laughed him out of patience; and that night

I laughed him into patience, and next morn.

Here the ninth hour I drunk him to his bed, then put my tires and mantles on him; whilst I wore his sword Philippan.

(Messenger enter)

Oh, from Italy

Ram thou thy fruitful tidings in mine ears, that long time have been barren.

Messenger: Madam, madam

Cleopatra: Antonius dead! If thou say so, villain, Thou kill'st thy mistress, but well and free, if thou so yield him there is gold, and here my bluest veins to kiss a hand that kings have lipped, and trembled kissing.

Messenger: First, madam, he is well.

Cleopatra: Why, there's more gold, but, sirrah, Mark, we use to say the dead are well, to bring it to that.

The gold I give thee will I melt and pour down thy ill-uttering throat.

Messenger: Good madam, hear me.

Cleopatra: Well, go to, I will.

Cleopatra: But there's no goodness in thy face, if Mark Anthony be free and healthful; so tart a favour to trumpet such good tidings! If not well, thou shouldst come like a Fury crowned with snakes, not like a formal man.

Messenger: Will it please you hear me?

Cleopatra: I have a mind to strike thee ere thou speak'st, yet if thou say Mark Anthony lives, is well, or friends with Caesar, or not captive to him; I'll set thee in a shower of gold, and hail rich pearls upon thee.

Messenger: Madam, he's well.

Cleopatra: Well said.

Messenger: And friends with Caesar.

Cleopatra: Thou'rt an honest man.

Messenger: Caesar and he are greater friends than ever.

Cleopatra: Make thee a fortune from me.

Messenger: But yet, madam.

Cleopatra: I do not like But yet, it does allay the good precedence; fire be set upon 'But yet'!
'But yet' is as a gaoler to bring forth some monstrous malefactor. Prithee, friend, pour out the pack of matter to mine ear, the good and bad together; he's friends with Caesar, in state of health thou say'st; and thou say'st free.

Messenger: Free, madam! No I made no such report. He's bound unto Octavia:

Cleopatra: For what good turn?

Messenger: For the best turn in the bed.

Cleopatra: I am pale, Charmain:

Messenger: Madam, he's married to Octavia.

Cleopatra: The most infectious pestilence upon thee!

(Cleopatra strikes Messenger down)

Messenger: Good madam, patience.

Cleopatra: What say you? Hence,

(Strikes him again)

Horrible villain! or I'll spurn thine eyes like balls before me, I'll unhair thy head:

(She hales him up and down)

Thou shalt be whipped with wire and stewed in brine smarting in lingering pickle.

Messenger: Gracious madam,

I that do bring the news made not the match.

Cleopatra: Say it is not so, a province I will give thee, and make thy fortunes proud; the blow thou hadst shall make thy peace for moving me to rage; and I will boot thee with what gift beside thy modesty can beg.

Messenger: He's married, madam.

Cleopatra: Rogue, thou hast lived too long.

(Draws a knife)

Messenger: Nay, then I'll run.

What mean you, madam? I have made no fault.

(Exits)

Charmain: Good madam, keep yourself within yourself:
The man is innocent.

Cleopatra: Some innocents escape not the thunderbolt.
Melt Egypt into Nile! and kindly creatures turn all to serpents!
Call the slave again though I am mad, I will not bite him.
Call him forth.

Charmain: He is afeard to come.

Cleopatra: I will not hurt him.

(Exit Charmain)

Cleopatra: These hands do lack nobility, that they strike a meaner than myself; since I myself

Have given myself the cause.

(Charmain and Messenger re-enters)

Come hither, sir.

Though it be honest, it is never good to bring bad news, give to a gracious message, and host of tongues; but let ill tidings tell themselves when they be felt.

Messenger: I have done my duty.

Cleopatra: Is he married?

I cannot hate thee worser than I do if thou again say 'Yes.'

Messenger: He's married, madam.

Cleopatra: The gods confound thee! Dost thou hold there still?

Messenger: Should I lie, madam?

Cleopatra: Oh, I would thou didst,

So half my Egypt were submerged and made a cistern for scaled snakes! Go, get thee hence hadst thou Narcissus in thy face, to me. Thou wouldst appear most ugly. He is married?

Messenger: I crave your highness' pardon.

Cleopatra: He is married?

Messenger: Take no offence that I would not offend you:

To punish me for what you make me do seems much unequal. He's married to Octavia.

Cleopatra: Oh, that his fault should make a knave of thee, that art not what thou'rt sure of!

Get thee hence the merchandise which thou hast brought from Rome Are all too dear for me, lie they upon thy hand, and be undone by them!

(Exit Messenger)

Charmain: Good your highness, patience.

Cleopatra: In praising Mark Anthony, I have dispraised Caesar.

Charmain: Many times, madam.

Cleopatra: I am paid for it now.

Lead me from hence I faint, Oh Iras, Charmain! It is no matter.

Go to the fellow good Alexas, bid him report the feature of Octavia; her years, her inclination, let him not leave out the colour of her hair: bring me word quickly.

(Exit Alexas)

Let him forever go, let him not, Charmain,

Though he be painted one way like a Gorgon, the other way's a Mars.

Bid you Alexas

(To Mardian)

Bring me word how tall she is.

Pity me, Charmain, but do not speak to me, lead me to my chamber.

(Exit)

Act II, Scene 6

Near Misenum.

(Flourish are delivered)

(Pompey and Menas at one door enter, with drum and trumpet at another door Octavius Caesar, Mark Anthony, Lepidus, Domitius Enobarbus, Mecaenas, with Soldiers marching enter)

Pompey: Your hostages I have, so have you mine and we shall talk before we fight.

Octavius: Most meet, that first we come to words; and therefore have we our written purposes before us sent; which, if thou hast considered let us know if it will tie up thy discontented sword, and carry back to Sicily much tall youth that else must perish here.

Pompey: To you all three, the senators alone of this great world; chief factors for the gods I do not know wherefore my father should revengers want.

Having a son and friends, since Julius Caesar, who at Philippi the good Brutus ghosted, there saw you labouring for him.

What was it that moved pale Cassius to conspire, and what made the all-honoured, honest Roman Brutus, with the armed rest, courtiers and beauteous freedom.

To drench the Capitol, but that they would have one man but a man? And that is it hath made me rig my navy, at whose burthen the angered ocean foams with which I meant to scourge the ingratitude that despiteful Rome cast on my noble father.

Octavius: Take your time.

Mark Anthony: Thou canst not fear us, Pompey, with thy sails we'll speak with thee at sea, at land.

Thou know'st how much we do over-count thee.

Pompey: At land, indeed, thou dost over-count me of my father's house, but, since the cuckoo builds not for himself, remain in it as thou mayst.

Lepidus: Be pleased to tell us, for this is from the present, how you take the offers we have sent you.

Octavius: There's the point.

Mark Anthony: Which do not be entreated to, but weigh what it is worth embraced.

Octavius: And what may follow, to try a larger fortune.

Pompey: You have made me offer of Sicily, Sardinia, and I must rid all the sea of pirates; then, to send measures of wheat to Rome; this agreed upon to part with unhacked edges, and bear back
Our targes undinted.

Octavius: (with Mark Anthony and Lepidus) That's our offer.

Pompey: Know then, I came before you here a man prepared to take this offer, but Mark Anthony put me to some impatience; though I lose the praise of it by telling, you must know, when Caesar and your brother were at blows your mother came to Sicily and did find her welcome friendly.

Mark Anthony: I have heard it, Pompey, and am well studied for a liberal thanks, which I do owe you.

Pompey: Let me have your hand, I did not think sir, to have met you here.

Mark Anthony: The beds in the east are soft; and thanks to you, that called me timelier than my purpose hither; for I have gained by it.

Octavius: Since I saw you last, there is a change upon you.

Pompey: Well, I know not what counts harsh fortune casts upon my face, but in my bosom shall she never come, to make my heart her vassal.

Lepidus: Well met here.

Pompey: I hope so Lepidus, thus we are agreed, I crave our composition may be written and sealed between us.

Octavius: That's the next to do.

Pompey: We'll feast each other ere we part; and let's
Draw lots who shall begin.

Mark Anthony: That will I Pompey.

Pompey: No, Mark Anthony, take the lot, but first or last your fine Egyptian cookery shall have the fame.
I have heard that Julius Caesar grew fat with feasting there.

Mark Anthony: You have heard much.

Pompey: I have fair meanings sir.

Mark Anthony: And fair words to them.

Pompey: Then so much have I heard, and I have heard, Apollodorus carried…

Domitius Enobarus: No more of that, he did so.

Pompey: What, I pray you?

Domitius Enobarus: A certain queen to Caesar in a mattress.

Pompey: I know thee now, how farest thou, soldier?

Domitius Enobarus: Well, and well am like to do, for I perceive four feasts are toward.

Pompey: Let me shake thy hand, I never hated thee; I have seen thee fight when I have envied thy behavior.

Domitius Enobarus: Sir, I never loved you much, but I had praised ye when you have well deserved ten times as much as I have said you did.

Pompey: Enjoy thy plainness, if nothing ill becomes thee, aboard my galley I invite you all.

Will you lead, lords?

Octavius: (with Mark Anthony and Lepidus)

Pompey: Come.

(Exit all but Menas and Enobarbus)

Menas: (From Aside) Thy father, Pompey, would never have made this treaty, you and I have known sir.

Domitius Enobarus: At sea, I think.

Menas: We have, sir.

Domitius Enobarus: You have done well by water.

Menas: And you by land.

Domitius Enobarus: I will praise any man that will praise me, though it cannot be denied what I have done by land.

Menas: Nor what I have done by water.

Domitius Enobarus: Yes, something you can deny for your own safety, you have been a great thief by sea.

Menas: And you by land.

Domitius Enobarus: There I deny my land service, but give me your hand Menas, if our eyes had authority; here they might take two thieves kissing.

Menas: All men's faces are true, whatsomever their hands are.

Domitius Enobarus: But there is never a fair woman has a true face.

Menas: No slander; they steal hearts.

Domitius Enobarus: We came hither to fight with you.

Menas: For my part, I am sorry it is turned to a drinking. Pompey doth this day laugh away his fortune.

Domitius Enobarus: If he do, sure, he cannot weep it back again.

Menas: You've said, sir. We looked not for Mark Anthony here, pray you, is he married to Cleopatra?

Domitius Enobarus: Caesar's sister is called Octavia.

Menas: True, sir; she was the wife of Caius Marcellus.

Domitius Enobarus: But she is now the wife of Marcus Antonius.

Menas: Pray yee, sir?

Domitius Enobarus: it is true.

Menas: Then is Caesar and he for ever knit together.

Domitius Enobarus: If I were bound to divine of this unity, I would not prophesy so.

Menas: I think the policy of that purpose made more in the marriage than the love of the parties.

Domitius Enobarus: I think so too, but you shall find the band that seems to tie their friendship together will be the very strangler of their amity; Octavia is of a wholesome, cold, and still conversation.

Menas: Who would not have his wife so?

Domitius Enobarus: Not he that himself is not so, which is Mark Anthony, he will to his Egyptian dish again; then shall the sighs of Octavia blow the fire up in Caesar.

And as I said before, that which is the strength of their amity shall prove the immediate author of their variance.

Mark Anthony will use his affection where it is he married but his occasion here.

Menas: And thus it may be. Come, sir, will you aboard? I have a health for you.

Domitius Enobarus: I shall take it, sir: we have used our throats in Egypt.

Menas: Come, let's away.

(Exit)

Act II, Scene 7

On board Pompey's galley, off Misenum.

(Music plays, two or three servants enter with a banquet)

First Servant: Here they'll be, man, some of their plants are ill-rooted already; the least wind in the world will blow them down.

Second Servant: Lepidus is high-coloured.

First Servant: They have made him drink alms-drink.

Second Servant: As they pinch one another by the disposition, he cries out "No more"; reconciles them to his entreaty whilst himself to the drink.

First Servant: It raises the greater war between him and his discretion.

Second Servant: Why, this is to have a name in great men's fellowship: I had as life have a reed that will do me no service as a partisan I could not heave.

First Servant: To be called into a huge sphere, and not to be seen to move in it, are the holes where eyes should be, which pitifully disaster the cheeks.

(A sennet sounded. Enter Octavius Caesar, Mark Anthony, Lepidus, Pompey, Agrippa, Mecaenas, Omitius Enobarbus, Menas, with other captains)

Mark Anthony: **(To Octavius Caesar)** Thus do they sir, they take the flow of the Nile by certain scales in the pyramid; they know, by the height, the lowness, or the mean, if death or poison follow.

The higher Nilus swells the more it promises, as it webs the seamen upon the slime and ooze, scattering Neptune's grain, and shortly comes to harvest.

Lepidus: You've strange serpents there.

Mark Anthony: Ay, Lepidus:

Lepidus: Your serpent of Egypt is bred now of your mud by the operation of your sun.

So is your crocodile.

Mark Anthony: They are so.

Pompey: Sit,—and some wine! A health to Lepidus!

Lepidus: I am not so well as I should be, but I'll never out.

Domitius Enobarus: Not till you have slept, I fear me you'll be in till then.

Lepidus: Nay, certainly, I have heard the Ptolemy's' pyramids are very goodly things; without contradiction, I have heard that.

Menas: (From Aside to Pompey) Pompey, a word.

Pompey: (From Aside to Menas) Say in mine ear, what is it?

Menas: (From Aside to Pompey) Forsake thy seat, I do beseech thee, captain, and hear me speak a word.

Pompey: (From Aside to Menas) Forbear me till anon this wine for Lepidus!

Lepidus: What manner of thing is your crocodile?

Mark Anthony: It is shaped, sir, like itself; and it is as broad as it hath breadth it is just so high as it is, and moves with its own organs;

it lives by that which nourisheth it, and the elements once out of it, it transmigrates.

Lepidus: What colour is it of?

Mark Anthony: Of it own colour too.

Lepidus: it is a strange serpent.

Mark Anthony: It is so. And the tears of it are wet.

Octavius: Will this description satisfy him?

Mark Anthony: With the health that Pompey gives him, else he is a very epicure.

Pompey: (From Aside to Menas) Go hang, sir, hang! Tell me of that? away!

Pompey: (From Aside to Menas) Go Do as I bid you, where's this cup I called for?

Menas: (From Aside to Pompey) If for the sake of merit thou wilt hear me, rise from thy stool.

Pompey: (From Aside to Menas) I think thou'rt mad. What is the matter?

(Rises, and walks From Aside)

Menas: I have ever held my cap off to thy fortunes.

Pompey: Thou hast served me with much faith. What's else to say? Be jolly, lords.

Mark Anthony: These quick-sands, Lepidus, keep off them for you sink.

Menas: Wilt thou be lord of all the world?

Pompey: What say'st thou?

Menas: Wilt thou be lord of the whole world? That's twice.

Pompey: How should that be?

Menas: But entertain it, and, though thou think me poor, I am the man will give thee all the world.

Pompey: Hast thou drunk well?

Menas: Now, Pompey, I have kept me from the cup.

Thou art, if thou darest be, the earthly love; whatever the ocean pales, or sky inclips is thine bidding, if thou wilt have it.

Pompey: Show me which way.

Menas: These three world-sharers, these competitors are in thy vessel, let me cut the cable, and, when we are put off, fall to their throats; all there is thine.

Pompey: Ah, this thou shouldst have done, and not have spoke on it! In me it is villainy, in thee't had been good service.

Thou must know, it is not my profit that does lead mine honour.

Pompey: Mine honour it, repent that ever thy tongue hath so betrayed thine act.

Being done unknown I should have found it afterwards, well done, but must condemn it now.

Desist, and drink.

Menas: (From Aside) For this, I'll never follow thy palled fortunes more.

Who seeks, and will not take when once it is offered, shall never find it more.

Pompey: This health to Lepidus!

Mark Anthony: Bear him ashore, I'll pledge it for him, Pompey.

Domitius Enobarus: Here's to thee, Menas!

Menas: Enobarbus, welcome!

Pompey: Fill till the cup be hid.

Domitius Enobarus: There's a strong fellow,

Menas: (Pointing to the Attendant who carries off Lepidus)

Menas: Why?

Domitius Enobarus: A' bears the third part of the world, man; see'st not?

Menas: The third part, then, is drunk: would it were all, that it might go on wheels!

Domitius Enobarus: Drink thou; increase the reels.

Menas: Come.

Pompey: This is not yet an Alexandrian feast.

Mark Anthony: It ripens towards it. Strike the vessels, oh?

Here is to Caesar!

Octavius: I could well forbear't.

It's monstrous labour, when I wash my brain,

And it grows fouler.

Mark Anthony: Be a child of the time.

Octavius: Possess it, I'll make answer, but I had rather fast from all four days than drink so much in one.

Domitius Enobarus: Ha, my brave emperor!

(To Mark Anthony)

Shall we dance now the Egyptian Bacchanals and celebrate our drink?

Pompey: Let's have it, good Soldier.

Mark Anthony: Come, let's all take hands, till that the conquering wine hath steeped our sense in soft and delicate Lethe.

Domitius Enobarus: All take hands.

Make battery to our ears with the loud music, the while I'll place you.

Then the boy shall sing, the holding every man shall bear as loud as his strong sides can volley.

(Music plays. Domitius Enobarbus places them hand in hand)
(Song)

Come, thou monarch of the vine, plumpy Bacchus with pink eyne!
In thy fats our cares be drowned, with thy grapes our hairs be crowned
Cup us, till the world go round,
Cup us, till the world go round!

Octavius: What would you more?

Pompey, good night. Good brother, let me request you off.

Our graver business frowns at this levity.

Gentle lords, let's part, you see we have burnt our cheeks, strong Enobarb is weaker than the wine; and mine own tongue splits what it speaks.

The wild disguise hath almost antick'd us all; what needs more words?

Good night.

Good Mark Anthony, your hand.

Pompey: I'll try you on the shore.

Mark Anthony: And shall, sir, give's your hand.

Pompey: Oh Mark Anthony,

You have my father's house, but, what? We are friends?

Come, down into the boat.

Domitius Enobarus: Take heed you fall not.

(Exit all but Domitius Enobarus and MENAS)

Menas, I'll not on shore.

Menas: No, to my cabin.

These drums! These trumpets, flutes! what!

Let Neptune hear we bid a loud farewell

To these great fellows: sound and be hanged, sound out! 1540

(Sound a flourish, with drums)

Domitius Enobarus: Oh! says ah There's my cap.

Menas: Oh! Noble captain, come.

(Exit)

Act III, Scene 1

A plain in Syria.

(Ventidius as it were in triumph, with Silius, and other Romans, Officers, and Soldiers; enter while the dead body of Pacorus borne before him)

Ventidius: Now, darting Parthia, art thou struck, and now pleased fortune does of Marcus Crassus' death make me revenger.

Bear the king's son's body before our army.

Thy Pacorus, Orodes, pays this for Marcus Crassus.

Silius: Noble Ventidius, whilst yet with Parthian blood thy sword is warm,

The fugitive Parthians follow, spur through Media, Mesopotamia, and the shelters whither the routed fly.

So thy grand captain Mark Anthony shall set thee on triumphant chariots and put garlands on thy head.

Ventidius: Oh Silius, Silius, I have done enough; a lower place, note well, may make too great an act, for learn this, Silius, better to leave undone than by our deed acquire too high a fame when him we serve's away.

Caesar and Mark Anthony have ever won more in their officer than person, Sossius, one of my place in Syria, his lieutenant; For quick accumulation of renown, which he achieved by the minute, lost his favour.

Who does in the wars more than his captain can becomes his captain's captain, and ambition, the soldier's virtue rather makes choice of loss than gain which darkens him.

I could do more to do Antonius good, but it would offend him and in his offence; should my performance perish.

Silius: Thou hast, Ventidius, that without the which a soldier and his sword grants scarce distinction, Thou wilt write to Mark Anthony!

Ventidius: I'll humbly signify what in his name that magical word of war we have effected; how with his banners and his well-paid ranks the never-yet-beaten horse of Parthia we have jaded out of the field.

Silius: Where is he now?

Ventidius: He purposeth to Athens, whither, with what haste the weight we must convey with what will permit; we shall appear before him.

On there; pass along!

(Exit)

Act III, Scene 2

An ante-chamber in Octavius Caesar's house. (Rome)

(Agrippa at one door, Domitius Enobarus at another, enter)

Agrippa: What, are the brothers parted?

Domitius Enobarus: They have dispatched with Pompey, he is gone; the other three are sealing.

Octavia weeps to part from Rome, Caesar is sad; and Lepidus; since Pompey's feast, as Menas says, is troubled with the green sickness.

Agrippa: it is a noble Lepidus:

Domitius Enobarus: A very fine one, Oh how he loves Caesar!

Agrippa: Nay, but how dearly he adores Mark Anthony!

Domitius Enobarus: Caesar? Why, he's the Jupiter of men.

Agrippa: What's Mark Anthony? The god of Jupiter.

Domitius Enobarus: Spake you of Caesar? How! The non-pareil!

Agrippa: Oh Mark Anthony! Oh thou Arabian bird!

Domitius Enobarus: Would you praise Caesar, say Caesar, go no further.

Agrippa: Indeed, he plied them both with excellent praises.

Domitius Enobarus: But he loves Caesar best; yet he loves Mark Anthony.

Oh! hearts, tongues, figures, scribes, bards, poets, cannot think, speak, cast, write, sing, number, oh!

His love to Mark Anthony, but as for Caesar, kneel down, kneel down, and wonder.

Agrippa: Both he loves.

Domitius Enobarus: They are his shards, and he their beetle.

(Trumpets within)

So his is to horse, Adieu noble Agrippa.

Agrippa: Good fortune, worthy soldier; and farewell.

(Octavius Caesar, Mark Anthony, Lepidus, and Octavia enter)

Mark Anthony: No further, sir.

Octavius: You take from me a great part of myself use me well in it Sister, prove such a wife as my thoughts make thee, and as my farthest band shall pass on thy approval of most noble Mark Anthony.

Let not the piece of virtue, which is set betwixt us, as the cement of our love.

To keep it builded, be the ram to batter the fortress of it, for better might we have loved without this mean, if on both parts this be not cherished.

Mark Anthony: Make me not offended in your distrust.

Octavius: I have said.

Mark Anthony: You shall not find, though you be therein curious, the least cause for what you seem to fear so.

The gods keep you, and make the hearts of Romans serve your ends! We will here part.

Octavius: Farewell, my dearest sister, fare thee well, the elements be kind to thee, and make thy spirits all of comfort!
Fare thee well.

Octavia: My noble brother!

Mark Anthony: The April's in her eyes: it is love's spring, and these the showers to bring it on.
Be cheerful.

Octavia: Sir, look well to my husband's house,,, and…

Octavius: What, Octavia?

Octavia: I'll tell you in your ear.

Mark Anthony: Her tongue will not obey her heart, nor can her heart inform her tongue, the swan's down-feather that stands upon the swell at full of tide; and neither way inclines.

Domitius Enobarus: (From Aside to Agrippa) Will Caesar weep?

Agrippa: (From Aside to Domitius Enobarus) He has a cloud in his face.

Domitius Enobarus: (From Aside to Agrippa) He were the worse for that, were he a horse; so is he being a man.

Agrippa: (From Aside to Domitius Enobarus): Why, Enobarbus,

Agrippa: (From Aside to Domitius Enobarus): When Mark Anthony found Julius Caesar dead, he cried almost to roaring; and he wept
when at Philippi he found Brutus slain.

Domitius Enobarus: (From Aside to Agrippa) That year, indeed, he was troubled with a rheum; what willingly he did confound he wailed, believe it, till I wept too.

Octavius: No, sweet Octavia,
You shall hear from me still, the time shall not out-go my thinking on you.

Mark Anthony: Come sir, come, I'll wrestle with you in my strength of love.

Look here, I have you thus, I let you go, and give you to the gods.

Octavius: Adieu; be happy!

Lepidus: Let all the number of the stars give light to thy fair way!

Octavius: Farewell, farewell!

(Kisses Octavia)

Mark Anthony: Farewell!

(Trumpets sound)

(Exit)

Act III, Scene 3

Cleopatra's palace. (Alexandria)

(Cleopatra, Charmain, IRAS, and Alexas enter)

Cleopatra: Where is the fellow?

Alexas: Half afeard to come.

Cleopatra: Go to, go to.

(Messenger enters)

Come hither, sir.

Alexas: Good majesty, Herod of Jewry dare not look upon you, but when you are well pleased.

Cleopatra: That Herod's head, I'll have, but how when Mark Anthony is gone through whom I might command it? Come thou near.

Messenger: Most gracious majesty…

Cleopatra: Didst thou behold Octavia?

Messenger: Ay, dread queen.

Cleopatra: Where?

Messenger: Madam, in Rome, I looked her in the face, and saw her led between her brother and Mark Anthony.

Cleopatra: Is she as tall as me?

Messenger: She is not, madam.

Cleopatra: Didst hear her speak? Is she shrill-tongued or low?

Messenger: Madam, I heard her speak, she is low-voiced.

Cleopatra: That's not so good, he cannot like her long.

Charmain: Like her! Oh Isis! It is impossible.

Cleopatra: I think so Charmain, dull of tongue, and dwarfish!

What majesty is in her gait? Remember,

If ever thou look'dst on majesty.

Messenger: She creeps, her motion and her station are as one.

She shows a body rather than a life, a statue than a breather.

Cleopatra: Is this certain?

Messenger: Or I have no observance.

Charmain: Three in Egypt cannot make better note.

Cleopatra: He's very knowing, I do perceive it, there's nothing in her yet: the fellow has good judgment.

Charmain: Excellent.

Cleopatra: Guess at her years, I prithee.

Messenger: Madam, she was a widow.

Cleopatra: Widow! Charmain, hark.

Messenger: And I do think she's thirty.

Cleopatra: Bear'st thou her face in mind? Is it long or round?

Messenger: Round even to faultiness.

Cleopatra: For the most part, too, they are foolish that are so.

Her hair, what colour?

Messenger: Brown, madam: and her forehead, as low as she would wish it.

Cleopatra: There's gold for thee.

Thou must not take my former sharpness ill, I will employ thee back again; I find thee most fit for business.

Go make thee ready, our letters are prepared.

(Messenger exits)

Charmain: A proper man.

Cleopatra: Indeed, he is so, I repent me much that so I harried him. Why, methinks, by him, this creature's no such thing.

Charmain: Nothing, madam.

Cleopatra: The man hath seen some majesty, and should know.

Charmain: Hath he seen majesty? Isis else defend, and serving you so long!

Cleopatra: I have one thing more to ask him yet, good Charmain, but it is no matter; thou shalt bring him to me
Where I will write. All may be well enough.

Charmain: I warrant you, madam.

(Exit)

Act III, Scene 4

A room in Mark Anthony's house. (Athens)

(Mark Anthony and Octavia enter)

Mark Anthony: Nay, nay, Octavia, not only that, that were excusable, that, and thousands more of semblable import; but he hath waged new wars against Pompey, made his will, and read it to public ear.

Spoke scantly of me, when perforce he could not but pay me terms of honour; cold and sickly he vented them, most narrow measure lent me when the best hint was given him, he not took it, or did it from his teeth.

Octavia: Oh my good lord, believe not all, or, if you must believe, stomach not All.

A more unhappy lady, if this division chance never stood between, praying for both parts.

Octavia: The good gods me presently when I shall pray, Oh bless my lord and husband!'

Undo that prayer, by crying out as loud, Oh bless my brother! Husband win, win brother, prays, and destroys the prayer; no midway it was these extremes at All:

Mark Anthony: Gentle Octavia, let your best love draw to that point, which seeks best to preserve it.

If I lose mine honour, I lose myself, better I were not yours than yours so branchless; but, as you requested, yourself shall go between 's the mean time.

Lady, I'll raise the preparation of a war and shall stain your brother, make your soonest haste, so your desires are yours.

Octavia: Thanks to my lord, the love of power make me most weak, most weak.

Your reconciler! Wars it was you twain would be, as if the world should cleave and that slain men should solder up the rift.

Mark Anthony: When it appears to you where this begins, turn your displeasure that way: for our faults, can never be so equal, that your love can equally move with them.

Provide you are going to choose your own company, and command what cost your heart has mind to.

(Exit)

Act III, Scene 5

The same general location. Another room.

(Domitius Enobarus and Eros enter, greeting)

Domitius Enobarus: How now, friend Eros!

Eros: There's strange news come, sir.

Domitius Enobarus: What, man?

Eros: Caesar and Lepidus have made wars upon Pompey.

Domitius Enobarus: This is old, what is the success?

Eros: Caesar, having made use of him in the wars against Pompey, presently denied him rivality would not let him partake in the glory of the action, and not resting here, accuses him of letters he had formerly wrote to Pompey, upon his own appeal seizes him.
So the poor third is up, till death enlarge his confine.

Domitius Enobarus: Then, world, thou hast a pair of chaps, no more, and throw between them all the food thou hast, they'll grind the one the other.
Where's Mark Anthony?

Eros: He's walking in the garden, thus, and spurns the rush that lies before him; cries, Fool Lepidus! And threats the throat of that his officer that murdered Pompey:

Domitius Enobarus: Our great navy's rigged.

Eros: For Italy and Caesar, more, Domitius; my lord desires you presently.
My news, I might have told hereafter.

Domitius Enobarus: It is, will be night, but let it be.
Bring me to Mark Anthony.

Eros: Come sir.

(Exit)

Act III, Scene 6

Octavius Caesar's house. (Rome)

(Octavius Caesar, Agrippa, and Mecaenas enter)

Octavius: Contemning Rome, he has done all this, and more in Alexandria: here's the manner of it.

In the market-place, on a tribunal silvered, Cleopatra and himself in chairs of gold 1were publicly enthroned, at the feet sat Caesarion, whom they call my father's son; and all the unlawful issue that their lust.

Since then hath made between them, unto her he gave the establishment of Egypt; made her of lower Syria, Cyprus, Lydia, absolute queen.

Mecaenas: This in the public eye?

Octavius: In the common show-place, where they exercise, his sons he there proclaimed the kings of kings.

Great Media, Parthia, and Armenia.

He gave to Alexander; to Ptolemy he assigned

Syria, Cilicia, and Phoenicia, she in the habiliments of the goddess Isis; that day appeared; and loft before gave audience; as it is reported so.

Mecaenas: Let Rome be thus Informed.

Agrippa: Who, queasy with his insolence, already will their good thoughts call from him.

Octavius: The people know it; and have now received his accusations.

Agrippa: Who does he accuse?

Octavius Caesar: And that, having in Sicily Sextus Pompeius spoiled, we had not rated him his part of the isle; then does he say he lent me some shipping unrestored.

Lastly, he frets that Lepidus of the triumvirate should be deposed, and being that we detain all his revenue.

Agrippa: Sir, this should be answered.

Octavius: it is done already, and the messenger gone I have told him Lepidus was grown too cruel; that he his high authority abused, and did deserve his change.

For what I have conquered, I grant him part; but then, in his Armenia, and other of his conquered kingdoms, I demand the like.

Mecaenas: He'll never yield to that.

Octavius: Nor must not then be yielded to in this.

(Enter Octavia with her entourage)

Octavia: Hail Caesar, and my lord! Hail, most dear Caesar!

Octavius: That ever I should call thee castaway!

Octavia: You have not called me so, nor have you cause.

Octavius: Why have you stolen upon us thus! You come not like Caesar's sister.

The wife of Mark Anthony should have an army for an usher, and the neighs of horse to tell of her approach long were she did appear; the trees by the way should have borne men and expectation fainted longing for what it had not.

Nay, the dust should have ascended to the roof of heaven, raised by your populous troops, but you are come a market-maid to Rome, and have prevented the ostentation of our love; which left unshown is often left unloved; we should have met you by sea and land, supplying every stage with an augmented greeting.

Octavia: Good my lord, to come thus was I not constantly encouraged, but did on my free will.

My lord, Mark Anthony, hearing that you prepared for war, acquainted my grieved ear withal; whereon, I begged his pardon for return.

Octavius: Which soon he granted, being an obstruct between his lust and him.

Octavia: Do not say so, my lord.

Octavius: I have eyes upon him, and his affairs come to me on the wind.

Where is he now?

Octavia: My lord, in Athens.

Octavius: No, my most wronged sister, Cleopatra hath nodded him to her.

He hath given his empire up to a whore who now are levying the kings of the earth for war; he hath assembled Bocchus the king of Libya; Archelaus of Cappadocia, Philadelphos king Of Paphlagonia, the Thracian king Adallas, King Malchus of Arabia, King of Pont, Herod of Jewry, Mithridates king of Comagene, Polemon and Amyntas, The kings of Mede and Lycaonia; with a more larger list of sceptres.

Octavia: Ay me, most wretched, that have my heart parted betwixt two friends that do afflict each other!

Octavius: Welcome hither:

Your letters did withhold our breaking forth, till we perceived both how you were wrong led, and we in negligent danger.

Cheer your heart, be you not troubled with the time, which drives over your content these strong necessities, but let determined things to destiny held unbewailed their way.

Welcome to Rome, nothing more dear to me, you are abused beyond the mark of thought: and the high gods to do you justice, make them ministers; of us and those that love you.

Best of comfort, and ever welcome to us.

Agrippa: Welcome, lady.

Mecaenas: Welcome, dear madam.

Each heart in Rome does love and pity you, only the adulterous Mark Anthony most large in his abominations turns you off and gives his potent regiment to an esteem that noises it against us.

Octavia: Is it so, sir?

Octavius: Most certain. Sister, welcome, pray you, be ever known to patience: my dear'st sister!

(Exit)

Act III, Scene 7

Mark Anthony's camp. (Near Actium)

(Cleopatra and Domitius Enobarus enter)

Cleopatra: I will be even with thee, doubt it not.

Domitius Enobarus: But why, why, why?

Cleopatra: Thou hast forspoke my being in these wars, and say'st it is not fit.

Domitius Enobarus: Well, is it, is it?

Cleopatra: If not denounced against us, why should not we be there in person?

Domitius Enobarus: (From Aside) Well, I could reply, if we should serve with horse and mares together; the horse were merely lost; the mares would bear, a soldier and his horse.

Cleopatra: What is it you say?

Domitius Enobarus: Your presence needs must puzzle Mark Anthony, take from his heart, take from his brain, from his time; what should not then be spared.
He is already traduced for levity and it is said in Rome that Photinus and in as much, your maids manage this war.

Cleopatra: Sink Rome and their tongues rot that speak against us! A charge we bear in the war, and, as the president of my kingdom will appear there for a man.
Speak not against it, I will not stay behind.

Domitius Enobarus: Nay, I have done.
Here comes the emperor.

(Mark Anthony and Canidius enter)

Mark Anthony: Is it not strange, Canidius, that from Tarentum and Brundusium he could so quickly cut the Ionian sea, and take in Toryne?

You have heard on it, sweet?

Cleopatra: Celerity is never more admired than by the negligent.

Mark Anthony: A good rebuke, which might have well becomed the best of men, to taunt at slackness.

Canidius, we will fight with him by sea.

Cleopatra: By sea! What else?

Canidius: Why will my lord do so?

Mark Anthony: For that he dares us to it.

Domitius Enobarus: So hath my lord dared him to single fight.

Canidius: Ay, and to wage this battle at Pharsalia, where Caesar fought with Pompey, but these offers which serve not for his vantage, be shaken off; and so should you.

Domitius Enobarus: Your ships are not well manned, your mariners are muleters, reapers, people ingross'd by swift impress; in Caesar's fleet are those that often have against Pompey fought.

Their ships are yare, yours, heavy.

No disgrace shall fall you for refusing him at sea at being prepared for land.

Mark Anthony: By sea, by sea.

Domitius Enobarus: Most worthy sir, you therein throw away the absolute soldiership you have by land; distract your army, which doth most consist of war-marked footmen; leave unexecuted your own renowned knowledge.

Quite, forego the way which promises assurance, and give up yourself merely to chance and hazard from firm security.

Mark Anthony: I'll fight at sea.

Cleopatra: I have sixty sails, Caesar none better.

Mark Anthony: Our overplus of shipping will we burn and, with the rest full-manned, from the head of Actium, beat the approaching Caesar; but if we fail, we then can do it at land.

(Messenger enters)

Thy business?

Messenger: The news is true, my lord; he is descried; Caesar has taken Toryne.

Mark Anthony: Can he be there in person? It is impossible. Strange that power should be.

Canidius, our nineteen legions thou shalt hold by land, and our twelve thousand horse we'll to our ship, Away, my Thetis!

(Soldier enters)

How now, worthy soldier?

Soldier: Oh noble emperor, do not fight by sea, trust not to rotten planks, do you misdoubt this sword and these my wounds?

Let the Egyptians and the Phoenicians go a-ducking; we have used to conquer, standing on the earth, and fighting foot to foot.

Mark Anthony: Well, well: away!

(Exit Mark Anthony, Queen Cleopatra, and Domitius Enobarbus)

Soldier: By Hercules, I think I am in the right.

Canidius: Soldier, thou art, but his whole action grows not in the power on it, so our leader's led, and we are women's men.

Soldier: You keep by land the legions and the horse whole, do you not?

Canidius: Marcus Octavius, Marcus Justeius, Publicola, and Caelius, are for sea; but we keep whole by land.
This speed of Caesar's carries beyond belief.

Soldier: While he was yet in Rome his power went out in such distractions as beguiled all spies.

Canidius: Who's his lieutenant, hear you?

Soldier: They say, one Taurus.

Canidius: Well I know the man.

(Messenger enters)

Messenger: The emperor calls Canidius.

Canidius: With news the time's with labour, and throes forth each minute some.

(Exit)

Act III, Scene 8

A plain near Actium.

(Enter Octavius Caesar, and Taurus, with his army, marching)

Octavius: Taurus!

Taurus: My lord?

Octavius: Strike not by land, keep whole, provoke not battle till we have done at sea.

Do not exceed the prescript of this scroll our fortune lies upon this jump.

(Exit)

Act III, Scene 9

Another part of the plain.

(Mark Anthony and Domitius Enobarbus enter)

Mark Anthony: Set we our squadrons on, beyond side of the hill in eye of Caesar's battle, from which place we may the number of the ships behold; and so proceed accordingly.

(Exit)

Act III, Scene 10

Another part of the plain.

(Candidius marcheth with his land army one way over the stage, and Taurus the lieutenant of Octavius Caesar, the other way. After their going in, is heard the noise of a sea-fight)

(Alarms. Domitius Enobarbus enter)

Domitius Enobarus: Naught, naught all, naught! I can behold no longer The Antoniad, the Egyptian admiral, with all their sixty, fly and turn the rudder; to see't mine eyes are blasted.

(Scarus enters)

Scarus: Gods and goddesses, all the whole synod of them!

Domitius Enobarus: What's thy passion!

Scarus: The greater cantle of the world is lost with very ignorance; we have kissed away Kingdoms and provinces.

Domitius Enobarus: How appears the fight?

Scarus: On our side like the tokened pestilence where death is sure. Yon ruined nag of Egypt, whom leprosy overtake! In the midst of the fight, when vantage like a pair of twins appeared, both as the same, or rather ours the elder, the breeze upon her, like a cow in June, hoists sails and flies.

Domitius Enobarus: That I beheld; mine eyes did sicken at the sight, and could not endure a further view.

Scarus: She once being loofed, the noble ruin of her magic, Mark Anthony, claps on his sea-wing, and, like a doting mallard leaves the fight in height; flies after her, I never saw an action of such shame.

Scarus: Experience, manhood, honour, never before did violate so itself.

Domitius Enobarus: Alack, alack!

(Enter Canidius)

Canidius: Our fortune on the sea is out of breath, and sinks most lamentably; had our general been what he knew himself, it had gone well,

Oh he has given example for our flight, most grossly, by his own!

Domitius Enobarus: Ay, are you thereabouts? Why then? Good night indeed.

Canidius: Toward Peloponnesus are they fled.

Scarus: it is easy to it; and there I will attend what further comes.

Canidius: To Caesar will I render my legions and my horse, six kings already

show me the way of yielding.

Domitius Enobarus: I'll yet follow, the wounded chance of Mark Anthony, though my reason sits in the wind against me.

(Exit)

Act III, Scene 11

Cleopatra's palace. (Alexandria)

(Mark Anthony enters with Attendants)

Mark Anthony: Hark! The land bids me tread no more upon it; it is ashamed to bear me!

Friends, come hither, I am so lated in the world, that I have lost my way for ever.

I have a ship aden with glold. take that, divide it, fly and make your peace with Caesar.

All: Fly! not we.

Mark Anthony: I have fled myself; and have instructed cowards to run and show their shoulders.

Friends be gone, I have myself resolved upon a course which has no need of you; be gone; my treasure's in the harbour, take it.

Oh, I followed that I blush to look upon my very hairs do mutiny, for the white reprove the brown for rashness, and they them for fear and doting.

Friends, be gone: you shall have letters from me to some friends that will sweep your way for you.

Pray you, look not sad, nor make replies of loathness, take the hint which my despair proclaims; let that be left which leaves itself to the sea-side straightway.

I will possess you of that ship and treasure. leave me, I pray, a little. Pray you now, nay, do so for indeed I have lost command; therefore I pray you I'll see you by and by.

(Sits down)

(Enter Cleopatra led by Chermain and Iras; Eros following)

Eros: Nay, gentle madam, to him, comfort him.

Iras: Do, most dear queen.

Charmain: Do! Why? What else?

Cleopatra: Let me sit down. Oh Juno!

Mark Anthony: No, no, no, no, no.

Eros: See you here, sir?

Mark Anthony: Oh fire, fire, fire!

Charmain: Madam!

Iras: Madam, Oh good empress!

Eros: Sir, sir

Mark Anthony: Yes, my lord, yes, he at Philippi kept his sword even like a dancer; while I struck the lean and wrinkled Cassius, and it was I that the mad Brutus ended.

He alone dealt on lieutenantry, and no practise had in the brave squares of war, yet now no matter.

Cleopatra: Ah, stand by.

Eros: The queen, my lord, the queen.

Iras: Go to him, madam, speak to him, he is unqualitied with very shame.

Cleopatra: Well then, sustain him: Oh!

Eros: Most noble sir, arise; the queen approaches, her head's declined, and death will seize her; but your comfort makes the rescue.

Mark Anthony: I have offended reputation, a most unnoble swerving.

Eros: Sir, the queen.

Mark Anthony: Of whither hast thou led me, Egypt? See how I convey my shame out of thine eyes by looking back what I have left behind destroyed in dishonour.

Cleopatra: Oh my lord, my lord.
Forgive my fearful sails! I little thought you would have followed.

Mark Anthony: Egypt, thou knew'st too well my heart was to thy rudder tied by the strings, and thou shouldst tow me after; over my spirit thy full supremacy thou knew'st, and that thy beck might from the bidding of the gods command me.

Cleopatra: Oh my pardon!

Mark Anthony: Now I must to the young man send humble treaties, dodge and palter in the shifts of lowness, who with half the bulk of the world played as I pleased; making and marring fortunes.
You did know how much you were my conqueror; and that my sword, made weak by my affection, would obey it on all cause.

Cleopatra: Pardon, pardon!

Mark Anthony: Fall not a tear, I say, one of them rates all that is won and lost; give me a kiss; even this repays me.
We sent our schoolmaster, is he come back? Love, I am full of lead. Some wine within there, and our meats! Fortune knows we scorn her most when most she offers blows.

(Exit)

Act III, Scene 12

Egypt. Octavius CAESAR's camp.

(Octavius Caesar, Dolabella, and Thyreus enter with others)

Octavius: Let him appear that's come from Mark Anthony: Know you him?

Dolabella: Caesar, it is his schoolmaster.

An argument that he is plucked when hither he sends so poor a pinion off his wing, which had superfluous kings for messengers, not many moons gone by.

(Euphronius, ambassador from Mark Anthony enter)

Octavius: Approach, and speak.

Euphronius: Such as I am, I come from Mark Anthony, I was of late as petty to his ends as is the morn-dew on the myrtle-leaf to his grand sea.

Octavius: Be it so, declare thine office.

Euphronius: Lord of his fortunes he salutes thee, and requires to live in Egypt, which not granted, he lessens his requests, and to thee sues to let him breathe between the heavens and earth, a private man in Athens.

This for him, next, Cleopatra does confess thy greatness; submits her to thy might, and of thee craves the circle of the Ptolemy for her heirs, now hazarded to thy grace.

Octavius: For Mark Anthony, I have no ears to his request.

The queen of audience nor desire shall fail, so she from Egypt drive her all-disgraced friend, or take his life there; this if she perform, she shall not sue unheard.

So to them both.

Euphronius: Fortune pursue thee!

Octavius: Bring him through the bands.

(Exit Euphronius)

(To Thyreus) To try eloquence, now it is time, dispatch.

From Mark Anthony win Cleopatra, promise and in our name, what she requires add more; from thine invention offers women are not in their best fortunes strong; but want will perjure the never touched vestal.

Try thy cunning, Thyreus; make thine own edict for thy pains, which we will answer as a law.

Thyreus: Caesar, I go.

Octavius: Observe how Mark Anthony becomes his flaw, and what thou think'st his very action speaks in every power that moves.

Thyreus: Caesar, I shall:

(Exit)

Act III, Scene 13

Cleopatra's palace. (Alexandria)

(Cleopatra, Domitius Enobarbus, Charmain, and Iras enter)

Cleopatra: What shall we do, Enobarbus?

Domitius Enobarus: Think, and die.

Cleopatra: Is Mark Anthony or we in fault for this?

Domitius Enobarus: Mark Anthony only, that would make his will lord of his reason.

What though, you fled from that great face of war, whose several ranges frighted each other?

Why should he follow? The itch of his affection should not then have nicked his captainship at such a point; when half to half the world opposed, he being the meered question.

It was a shame no less, than was his loss, to course your flying flags, and leave his navy gazing.

Cleopatra: Prithee, peace.

(Mark Anthony with Euphronius, the Ambassador enter)

Mark Anthony: Is that his answer?

Euphronius: Ay, my lord.

Mark Anthony: The queen shall then have courtesy, so she will yield us up.

Euphronius: He says so.

Mark Anthony: Let her know it, to the boy Caesar send this grizzled head, and he will fill thy wishes to the brim with principalities.

Cleopatra: That head, my lord?

Mark Anthony: To him again: tell him he wears the rose of youth upon him; from which the world should note something particular; his coin, ships, legions, may be a coward's; whose ministers would prevail ender the service of a child

Mark Anthony: As soon as is the command of Caesar, I dare him therefore to lay his gay comparisons apart, and answer me declined, sword against sword.

Ourselves alone, I'll write it, follow me.

(Exit Mark Anthony and Euphronius)

Domitius Enobarus: (From Aside) Yes, like enough, high-battled Caesar will unstate his happiness, and be staged to the show against a sworder!

I see men's judgments are a parcel of their fortunes; and things outward do draw the inward quality after them; to suffer all alike. That he should dream, knowing all measures, the full Caesar will answer his emptiness!

Caesar, thou hast subdued his judgment too.

(Attendant enter)

Attendant: A messenger from Caesar.

Cleopatra: What, no more ceremony? See, my women!

Against the blown rose may they stop their nose that kneeled unto the buds.

Admit him, sir.

(Exit Attendant)

Domitius Enobarus: (From Aside) Mine honesty and I begin to square.

The loyalty well held to fools does make our faith mere folly, yet he that can endure to follow with allegiance a fallen lord, does conquer him that did his master conquer, and earns a place in the story.

(Thyreus enters)

Cleopatra: Caesar's will?

Thyreus: Hear it apart.

Cleopatra: None but friends: say boldly.

Thyreus: So happily are they friends to Mark Anthony.

Domitius Enobarus: He needs as many sir, as Caesar has, or needs not us.

If Caesar please, our master will leap to be his friend for us.

You know whose he is we are, and that is, Caesar's.

Thyreus: So.

Thus then, thou most renowned, Caesar entreats, not to consider in what case thou stand'st; further than he is Caesar.

Cleopatra: Go on: right royal.

Thyreus: He knows that you embrace not Mark Anthony, as you did love, but as you feared him.

Cleopatra: Oh!

Thyreus: The scars upon your honour, therefore, he does pity, as consents our agree, with blemishes not as deserved.

Cleopatra: He is a god, and knows what is most right, mine honour was not yielded, but conquered merely.

Domitius Enobarus: (From Aside) To be sure of that, I will ask Mark Anthony.

Sir, sir, thou art so leaky, that we must leave thee to thy sinking, for thy dearest quit thee.

(Exit)

Thyreus: Shall I say to Caesar what you require of him? For he partly begs to be desired to give.

It much would please him, that of his fortunes you should make a staff to lean upon, but it would warm his spirits to hear from me you had left Mark Anthony and put yourself under his shrowd as the universal landlord.

Cleopatra: What's your name?

Thyreus: My name is Thyreus.

Cleopatra: Most kind messenger,

Cleopatra: Say to great Caesar this, in deputation I kiss his conquering hand; tell him, I am prompt to lay my crown at his feet, and there to kneel.

Tell him from his all-obeying breath I hear the doom of Egypt.

Thyreus: It is your noblest course, wisdom and fortune combating together; if that the former dare but what it can no chance may shake it.

Give me grace to lay my duty on your hand.

Cleopatra: Your Caesar's father oft, when he hath mused of taking kingdoms in, bestowed his lips on that unworthy place, as it rained kisses.

(Mark Anthony and Domitius Enobarbus re-enter)

Mark Anthony: Favours, by Jupiter that thunders!
What art thou, fellow?

Thyreus: One that but performs the bidding of the fullest man, and worthiest to have command obeyed.

Domitius Enobarus: (From Aside) You will be whipped.

Mark Anthony: Approach, there! Ah, you kite! Now, gods and devils!
Authority melts from me: of late, when I cried 'oh!'
Like boys unto a muss, kings would start forth, and cry 'Your will?'
Have you no ears?
I am Mark Anthony yet.

(Enter Attendants)

Take hence this Jack, and whip him.

Domitius Enobarus: (From Aside) it is better playing with a lion's whelp than with an old one dying.

Mark Anthony: Moon and stars!
Whip him, were it twenty of the greatest tributaries
That do acknowledge Caesar, should I find them so saucy with the hand of she here, what's her name, since she was Cleopatra?

Mark Anthony: Whip him, fellows, till, like a boy you see him cringe his face, and whine aloud for mercy; take him hence.

Thyreus: Mark Anthony!

Mark Anthony: Tug him away, being whipped, bring him again; this Jack of Caesar's shall bear us an errand to him.

(Exit Attendants with Thyreus)

You were half blasted ere I knew you, ha!

Have I my pillow left unpressed in Rome, forborne the getting of a lawful race, and by a gem of women, to be abused by one that looks on feeders?

Cleopatra: Good my lord.

Mark Anthony: You have been a boggler ever, but when we in our viciousness grow hard, Oh misery on it!

The wise gods seal our eyes, in our own filth drop our clear judgments, make us adore our errors; laugh at us while we strut to our confusion.

Cleopatra: Oh, is it come to this?

Mark Anthony: I found you as a morsel cold upon dead Caesar's trencher, nay, you were a fragment of Cneius Pompey's; besides what hotter hours unregister'd in vulgar fame.

You have luxuriously picked out, for I am sure, though you can guess what temperance should be; you know not what it is.

Cleopatra: Wherefore is this?

Mark Anthony: To let a fellow that will take rewards, and say 'God quit you!' be familiar with my playfellow, your hand; this kingly seal and plighted of high hearts!

Mark Anthony: Oh, that I were upon the hill of Basan, to outroar the horned herd! For I have savage cause, and to proclaim it civilly were like a haltered neck which does the hangman thank for being yare about him.

(Attendants with Thyreus re-enter)

Is he whipped?

First Attendant: Soundly, my lord.

Mark Anthony: Cried he? And begged a' pardon?

First Attendant: He did ask favour.

Mark Anthony: If that thy father live, let him repent; thou was it not made his daughter; and be thou sorry to follow Caesar in his triumph, since thou hast been whipped for following him Henceforth, the white hand of a lady fever thee, shake thou to look on it, get thee back to Caesar, tell him thy entertainment look, thou say he makes me angry with him; for he seems proud and disdainful, harping on what I am not, what he knew I was.

He makes me angry, and at this time most easy it is to do it, when my good stars, that were my former guides, have empty left their orbs, and shot their fires into the abysm of hell.

If he mislike my speech and what is done, tell him he has Hipparchus, my enfranched bondman, whom he may at pleasure whip, or hang, or torture, as he shall like, to quit me.

Urge it thou.

Hence with thy stripes, be gone.

(Exit Thyreus)

Cleopatra: Have you done yet?

Mark Anthony: Alack, our terrene moon is now eclipsed, and it portends alone the fall of Mark Anthony!

Cleopatra: I must stay his time.

Mark Anthony: To flatter Caesar, would you mingle eyes with one that ties his points?

Cleopatra: Not know me yet?

Mark Anthony: Cold-hearted toward me?

Cleopatra: Ah dear, if I be so, from my cold heart let heaven engender hail, and poison it in the source; and the first stone drop in my neck, as it determines so dissolve my life!

The next Caesarion smite! till by degrees the memory of my womb, together with my brave Egyptians all, by the discandying of this pelleted storm; lie graveless till the flies and gnats of Nile have buried them for prey!

Mark Anthony: I am satisfied.

Caesar sits down in Alexandria where I will oppose his fate.

Our force by land Hath nobly held, our severed navy too have knit again, and fleet, threatening most sea-like.

Where hast thou been, my heart? Dost thou hear, lady? If from the field I shall return once more to kiss these lips, I will appear in blood; I and my sword will earn our chronicle.

There's hope in it yet.

Cleopatra: That's my brave lord!

Mark Anthony: I will be treble-sinewed, hearted, breathed, and fight maliciously.

For when mine hours were nice and lucky, men did ransom lives of me for jests, but now I'll set my teeth and send to darkness all that stop me.

Come, let's have one other gaudy night, call to me, all my sad captains; fill our bowls once more, let's mock the midnight bell.

Cleopatra: It is my birth-day, I had thought to have held it poor; but since my lord is Mark Anthony again, I will be Cleopatra.

Mark Anthony: We will yet do well.

Cleopatra: Call all his noble captains to my lord.

Mark Anthony: Do so, we'll speak to them; and to-night I'll force the wine peep through their scars.

Come on, my queen, there's sap in it yet.

The next time I do fight, I'll make death love me; for I will contend even with his pestilent scythe.

(Exit all but Domitius Enobarus)

Domitius Enobarus: Now he'll outstare the lightning.

To be furious is to be frighted out of fear, and in that mood the dove will peck the estridge; and I see still a diminution in our captain's brain restores his heart.

When valour preys on reason, it eats the sword it fights with, I will seek some way to leave him.

(Exit)

Act IV, Scene 1

Octavius CAESAR's camp. (Before Alexandria)

(Octavius Caesar, Agrippa, and Mecaenas enter with his Army, Octavius Caesar is reading a letter)

Octavius: He calls me boy; and chides, as he had power to beat me out of Egypt; my messenger he hath whipped with rods; dares me to personal combat.

Caesar to Mark Anthony, let the old ruffian know I have many other ways to die; meantime laugh at his challenge.

Mecaenas: Caesar must think when one so great begins to rage, he's hunted even to falling.

Give him no breath, but now make boot of his distraction, never anger made good guard for itself.

Octavius: Let our best heads know that to-morrow the last of many battles we mean to fight, within our files there are, of those that served Mark Anthony; but late enough to fetch him in.

See it done and feast the army, we have store to do it and they have earned the waste. Poor Mark Anthony!

(Exit)

Act IV, Scene 2

Cleopatra's palace. (Alexandria)

(Mark Anthony, Cleopatra, Domitius Enobarbus, Charmain, Iras, Alexas, enter with others)

Mark Anthony: He will not fight with me, Domitius.

Domitius Enobarus: No.

Mark Anthony: Why should he not?

Domitius Enobarus: He thinks, being twenty times of better fortune, he is twenty men to one.

Mark Anthony: To-morrow, soldier, by sea and land I'll fight; or I will live, or bathe my dying honour in the blood.
Shall make it live again, Woo it thou fight well?

Domitius Enobarus: I'll strike, and cry Take All.

Mark Anthony: Well said, come on, call forth my household servants.
Let's to-night be bounteous at our meal.

(Enter three or four Servitors)

Give me thy hand, thou hast been rightly honest, so hast thou.
Thou, and thou, and thou, you have served me well, and kings have been your fellows.

Cleopatra: (From Aside to Domitius Enobarus) What means this?

Domitius Enobarus: (From Aside to Cleopatra) it is one of those odd tricks which sorrow shoots out of the mind.

Mark Anthony: And thou art honest too, I wish I could be made so many men, and all of you clapped up together in a Mark Anthony; that I might do you service.

So good as you have done.

All: The gods forbid!

Mark Anthony: Well, my good fellows, wait on me to-night, scant not my cups, and make as much of me as when mine empire was your fellow too; and suffered my command.

Cleopatra: (From Aside to Domitius Enobarus) What does he mean?

Domitius Enobarus: (From Aside to Cleopatra) To make his followers weep.

Mark Anthony: Tend me to-night, may be it is the period of your duty, happily you shall not see me more; or if a mangled shadow perchance to-morrow, you'll serve another master.

I look on you as one that takes his leave.

Mine honest friends I turn you not away, but, like a master Married to your good service, stay till death.

Tend me to-night two hours, I ask no more, and the gods yield you for it!

Domitius Enobarus: What mean you, sir, to give them this discomfort?

Look, they weep, and I, an ass, am onion-eyed for shame; transform us not to women.

Mark Anthony: Oh, oh, oh!

Now the witch take me, if I meant it thus!

Grace grow where those drops fall!

My hearty friends, you take me in too dolorous a sense; for I spake to you for your comfort; did desire you to burn this night with torches.

Know my hearts, I hope well of to-morrow and will lead you where rather I'll expect victorious life then death and honour.

Let's to supper, come, and drown consideration.

(Exit)

Act IV, Scene 3

The same general location. Before the palace.

(Two Soldiers to their guard enter)

First Soldier: Brother, good night: to-morrow is the day.

Second Soldier: It will determine one way: fare you well. Heard you of nothing strange about the streets?

First Soldier: Nothing. What news?

Second Soldier: Belike it is but a rumour, good night to you.

First Soldier: Well, sir, good night.

(Enter two other Soldiers)

Second Soldier: Soldiers, have careful watch.

Third Soldier: And you. Good night, good night.

(They place themselves in every corner of the stage)

Fourth Soldier: Hear we, and if to-morrow, our navy thrives, I have an absolute hope our landmen will stand up.

Third Soldier: it is a brave army, and full of purpose.

(Music of the hautboys as under the stage)

Fourth Soldier: Peace! What noise?

First Soldier: List, list!

Second Soldier: Hark!

First Soldier: Music in the air.

Third Soldier: Under the earth.

Fourth Soldier: It signs well, does it not?

Third Soldier: No.

First Soldier: Peace, I say!

What should this mean?

Second Soldier: it is the god Hercules, whom Mark Anthony loved, now leaves him.

First Soldier: Walk; let's see if other watchmen, do hear what we do?

(They advance to another post)

Second Soldier: How now, masters!

All: (Speaking together) How now!

How now! Do you hear this?

First Soldier: Ay; is it not strange?

Third Soldier: Do you hear, masters? Do you hear?

First Soldier: Follow the noise so far as we have quarter;

Let's see how it will give off.

All: Content. it is strange.

(Exit)

Act IV, Scene 4

The same general location. A room in the palace.

(Mark Anthony and Cleopatra enter, Charmain and others attending enter)

Mark Anthony: Eros! mine armour, Eros!

Cleopatra: Sleep a little.

Mark Anthony: No, my chuck. Eros, come; mine armour, Eros!

(Eros enters with armour)

Come good fellow, put mine iron on, if fortune be not ours to-day, it is because we brave her; come.

Cleopatra: Nay, I'll help too.

What's this for?

Mark Anthony: Ah, let be, let be! Thou art

The armourer of my heart: false, false; this, this.

Cleopatra: Sooth, la, I'll help: thus it must be.

Mark Anthony: Well, well;

We shall thrive now. Seest thou, my good fellow?

Go put on thy defences.

Eros: Briefly, sir.

Cleopatra: Is not this buckled well? 2635

Mark Anthony: Rarely, rarely.

He that unbuckles this, till we do please to dafft for our repose, shall hear a storm.

Thou fumblest, Eros; and my queen's a squire more tight at this than thou: dispatch.

Oh love, that thou couldst see my wars to-day, and knew'st the royal occupation!

Thou shouldst see a workman in it.

(Enter an armed Soldier)

Good morrow to thee, welcome, thou look'st like him that knows a warlike charge.

To business that we love we rise betime and go to it with delight.

Soldier: A thousand, sir, early though it be, have on their riveted trim; and at the port expect you.

(Shout. Trumpets flourish)

(Enter Captains and Soldiers)

Captain: The morn is fair. Good morrow, general.

All: Good morrow, general.

Mark Anthony: It is well blown, lads.

This morning, like the spirit of a youth, that means to be of note, begins betimes.

So, so, come, give me that, this way well said.

Fare thee well, dame; whatever becomes of me.

This is a soldier's kiss; rebukeable

(Kisses her)

And worthy shameful cheque it were, to stand on more mechanic compliment; I'll leave thee now, like a man of steel.

You that will fight, follow me close; I'll bring you to it. Adieu.

(Exit Mark Anthony, Eros, Captains, and Soldiers)

Charmain: Please you, retire to your chamber.

Cleopatra: Lead me, he goes forth gallantly.

That he and Caesar might determine this great war in single fight!

Then Mark Anthony, but now, well, on.

(Exit)

Act IV, Scene 5

Alexandria. Mark Anthony's camp.

(Trumpets sounds)

(Mark Anthony and Eros enter with Soldier meeting them)

Soldier: The gods make this a happy day to Mark Anthony!

Mark Anthony: Would thou and those thy scars had once prevailed, to make me fight at land!

Soldier: Hadst thou done so, the kings that have revolted, and the soldier that has this morning left thee, would have still followed thy heels.

Mark Anthony: Who's gone this morning?

Soldier: Who! One ever near thee call for Enobarbus, he shall not hear thee, or from Caesar's camp.

Saying I am none of thine.

Mark Anthony: What say'st thou?

Soldier: Sir, he is with Caesar.

Eros: Sir, his chests and treasure he has not with him.

Mark Anthony: Is he gone?

Soldier: Most certain.

Mark Anthony: Go, Eros, send his treasure after; do it. Detain no jot, I charge thee, write to him; I will subscribe gentle adieus and greetings.

Say that I wish he never find more cause to change a master, oh my fortunes have corrupted honest men!

Dispatch Enobarbus!

(Exit)

Act IV, Scene 6

Octavius Caesar's camp. (Alexandria)

(Flourish delivered)

(Octavius Caesar, Agrippa, with Domitius Enobarbus, and others enter)

Octavius: Go forth, Agrippa, and begin the fight, our will is Mark Anthony he look alive; make it so known.

Agrippa: Caesar, I shall.

(Exits)

Octavius: The time of universal peace is near; prove this a prosperous day, the civilized world shall bear the olive freely.

(Messenger enters)

Messenger: Mark Anthony is come into the field.

Octavius: Go charge Agrippa.

Plant those that have revolted in vain, that Mark Anthony may seem to spend his fury

upon himself.

(Exit all but Domitius Enobarus)

Domitius Enobarus: Alexas did revolt; and went to Jewry on affairs of Mark Anthony; there did persuade Great Herod to incline himself to Caesar and leave his master Mark Anthony.

For this pains Caesar, Caesar hath hanged him; Canidius and the rest that fell away have entertainment, but no honourable trust.

I have done ill, of which I do accuse myself so sorely, that I will joy no more.

(Enter a Soldier of Caesar's)

Soldier: Enobarbus, Mark Anthony hath after thee sent all thy treasure, with his bounty overplus; the messenger came on my guard; and at thy tent is now unloading of his mules.

Domitius Enobarus: I give it you.

Soldier: Mock not, Enobarbus, I tell you true; best you safed the bringer out of the host.

I must attend mine office, or would have done it myself; your emperor continues still a Jupiter.

(Exits)

Domitius Enobarus: I am alone the villain of the earth and feel I am so most.

Oh Mark Anthony, thou mine of bounty, how wouldst thou have paid my better service, when my turpitude thou dost so crown with gold!

This blows my heart, if swift thought break it not, a swifter mean shall outstrike thought, but thought will do it, I feel.

I fight against thee! No, I will go seek some ditch wherein to die the foul'st best fits my latter part of life.

(Exits)

Act IV, Scene 7

Field of battle between the camps.

(Alarms. Drums and trumpets)

(Agrippa and others enter)

Agrippa: Retire, we have engaged ourselves too far. Caesar himself has work, and our oppression exceeds what we expected.

(Exit)

(Alarmss)

(Mark Anthony and Scarus wounded enter)

Scarus: Oh my brave emperor, this is fought indeed! Had we done so at first, we had droven them home with clouts about their heads.

Mark Anthony: Thou bleed'st apace.

Scarus: I had a wound here that was like a T, but now it is made an H.

Mark Anthony: They do retire.

Scarus: We'll beat 'em into bench-holes, I have yet room for six scotches more.

(Enter Eros)

Eros: They are beaten, sir, and our advantage serves for a fair victory.

Scarus: Let us score their backs and snatch them up, as we take hares, behind.

It is sport to maul a runner.

Mark Anthony: I will reward thee once for thy spritely comfort, and ten-fold for thy good valour. Come thee on.

Scarus: I'll halt after.

(Exit)

Act IV, Scene 8

Under the walls of Alexandria.

(Alarms)

Mark Anthony enters in a march, Scarus enter with others)

Mark Anthony: We have beat him to his camp, run one before and let the queen know of our guests.

To-morrow, before the sun shall see 's, we'll spill the blood that has to-day escaped.

I thank you all for doughty-handed are you, and have fought tot as you served the cause, but as it had been each man's like mine you have shown all Hectors.

Enter the city, clip your wives, your friends, tell them your feats whilst they with joyful tears wash the congealment from your wounds; and kiss the honoured gashes whole.

Mark Anthony: (To Scarus)

Give me thy hand

(Cleopatra enters attended).

To this great fairy I'll commend thy acts, make her thanks bless thee.

(To Cleopatra)

Oh thou day of the world, Chain mine armed neck; leap thou, attire and all through proof of harness to my heart, and there ride on the pants triumphing!

Cleopatra: Lord of lords!

Oh infinite virtue, comest thou smiling from the world's great snare uncaught?

Mark Anthony: My nightingale, we have beat them to their beds. What, woman! Though grey do something mingle with our younger brown, yet have we a brain that nourishes our nerves, and can get goal for goal of youth.

Behold this man commend unto his lips thy favouring hand, kiss it, my warrior; he hath fought to-day as if a god, in hate of mankind, had destroyd in such a shape.

Cleopatra: I'll give thee, friend, an armour all of gold; it was a king's.

Mark Anthony: He has deserved it, were it carbuncled like holy Phoebus' car.

Give me thy hand, through Alexandria make a jolly march; bear our hacked targets like the men that owe them.

Had our great palace the capacity to camp this host, we all would supper together and drink carouses to the next day's fate; which promises royal peril.

Trumpeters, with brazen din blast you the city's ear, make mingle with rattling tabourines; that heaven and earth may strike their sounds together applauding our approach.

(Exit)

Act IV, Scene 9

Octavius Caesar's camp.

(Sentinels at their post)

First Soldier: If we be not relieved within this hour, we must return to the court of guard. The night is shiny, and they say we shall embattle by the second hour in the morn.

Second Soldier: This last day was a shrewd one to, was.

(Domitius Enobarus enter)

Domitius Enobarus: Oh bear me witness, night…

Third Soldier: What man is this?

Second Soldier: Stand close, and list him.

Domitius Enobarus: Be witness to me, Oh thou blessed moon, when men revolted shall upon record, bear hateful memory, poor Enobarbus did before thy face repent!

First Soldier: Enobarbus!

Third Soldier: Peace!

Hark further.

Domitius Enobarus: Oh sovereign mistress of true melancholy, the poisonous damp of night disponge upon me; that life, a very rebel to my will, may hang no longer on me.

Throw my heart against the flint and hardness of my fault, which being dried with grief, will break to powder and finish all foul thoughts.

Oh Mark Anthony, nobler than my revolt is infamous, forgive me in thine own particular; but let the world rank me in register a master-leaver and a fugitive.

Oh Mark Anthony! Oh Mark Anthony!

(Dies)

Second Soldier: Let's speak to him.

First Soldier: Let's hear him, for the things he speaks may concern Caesar.

Third Soldier: Let's do so. But he sleeps.

First Soldier: Swoons rather; for so bad a prayer as his was never yet for sleep.

Second Soldier: Go we to him.

Third Soldier: Awake, sir, awake; speak to us.

Second Soldier: Hear you, sir?

First Soldier: The hand of death hath caught him.

(Drums afar off)

Hark! The drums

Demurely wake the sleepers. Let us bear him to the court of guard, he is of note.

Our hour is fully out.

Third Soldier: Come on, then, he may recover yet.

(Exit with the body)

Act IV, Scene 10

Between the two camps.

(Enter Mark Anthony and Scarus, with their Army)

Mark Anthony: Their preparation is to-day by sea, we please them not by land.

Scarus: For both, my lord.

Mark Anthony: I would they would fight in the fire or in the air; we would fight there too, but this it is our foot upon the hills adjoining to the city shall stay with us.

Order for sea is given, they have put forth the haven where their appointment we may best discover, and look on their endeavour.

(Exit)

Act IV, Scene 11

Another part of The same general location.

(Octavius Caesar, and his Army enter)

Octavius: But being charged we will be still by land, which as I take it we shall; for his best force is forth to man his galleys.

To the vales, and hold our best advantage.

(Exit)

Act IV, Scene 12

Another part of The same general location.

(Enter Mark Anthony and Scarus)

Mark Anthony: Yet they are not joined where beyond pine does stand, I shall discover all; I'll bring thee word straight, how it is like to go.

(Exits)

Scarus: Swallows have built in Cleopatra's sails their nests, the augurers say they know not, they cannot tell.

Look grimly and dare not speak their knowledge.

Mark Anthony is valiant, and dejected; and by starts his fretted fortunes give him hope, and fear of what he has, and has not.

(Alarms afar off, as at a sea-fight)

(Mark Anthony re-enters)

Mark Anthony: All is lost; this foul Egyptian hath betrayed me.

My fleet hath yielded to the foe; and beyonder they cast their caps up and carouse together like friends long lost.

Triple-turned whore! Art thou.

Hast sold me to this novice, and my heart makes only wars on thee; bid them all fly for when I am revenged upon my charm I have done all.

Bid them all fly, begone.

(Scarus exits)

Oh sun, thy uprise shall I see no more fortune and Mark Anthony part here; even here do we shake hands.

All come to this? The hearts that spanieled me at heels, to whom I gave their wishes, do discandy, melt their sweets on blossoming Caesar; and this pine is barked that overtopped them all.

Betrayed I am, Oh this false soul of Egypt! This grave charm whose eye becked forth my wars, and called them home; whose bosom was my crownet, my chief end.

Like a right gipsy, hath, at fast and loose, beguiled me to the very heart of loss.

What, Eros, Eros!

(Enter Cleopatra)

Ah, thou spell! Avaunt!

Cleopatra: Why is my lord enraged against his love?

Mark Anthony: Vanish, or I shall give thee thy deserving, and blemish Caesar's triumph.

Let him take thee, and hoist thee up to the shouting plebeians.

Mark Anthony: Follow his chariot, like the greatest spot of all thy sex most monster-like be shown; for poor'st diminutives, for right; and let patient Octavia plough thy visage up with her prepared nails.

(Exit Cleopatra)

It is well thou'rt gone, if it be well to live, but better It were thou fell'st into my fury; for one death might have prevented many.

Eros, oh!

The shirt of Nessus is upon me.

Teach me Alcides, thou mine ancestor, thy rage; let me lodge Lichas on the horns of the moon, and with those hands that grasped the heaviest club subdue my worthiest self.

The witch shall die, to the young Roman boy she hath sold me, and I fall under this plot; she dies for it. Eros, oh!

(Exit)

Act IV, Scene 13

Cleopatra's palace. (Alexandria)

(Cleopatra, Charmain, Iras, and Mardian enter)

Cleopatra: Help me, my women! Oh he is more mad than Telamon for his shield; the boar of Thessaly was never so embossed.

Charmain: To the monument!

There lock yourself, and send him word you are dead.

The soul and body rive not more in parting than greatness going off.

Cleopatra: To the monument!

Mardian, go tell him I have slain myself; say, that the last I spoke was Mark Anthony.

And word it, prithee, piteously, hence, Mardian, and bring me how he takes my death.

To the monument!

(Exit)

Act IV, Scene 14

The same general location. Another room.

(Mark Anthony and Eros enter)

Mark Anthony: Eros, thou yet behold'st me?

Eros: Ay, noble lord.

Mark Anthony: Sometimes we see a cloud that's dragonish; A vapour sometime like a bear or lion, A towered citadel, a pendent rock, A forked mountain, or blue promontory
With trees upon it, that nod unto the world, and mock our eyes with air.
Thou hast seen these signs; they are black vesper's pageants.

Eros: Ay, my lord,

Mark Anthony: That which is now a horse, even with a thought the rack dislimns, and makes it indistinct as water is in water.

Eros: It does, my lord.

Mark Anthony: My good knave Eros, now thy captain is even such a body, here I am **Mark Anthony:** Yet cannot hold this visible shape, my knave.
I made these wars for Egypt, and the queen, whose heart I thought I had for she had mine; which whilst it was mine had annexed unto it a million more, now lost.
She, Eros, has packed cards with Caesar, and false-played my glory unto an enemy's triumph.
Nay, weep not gentle Eros; there is left us ourselves to end ourselves.

(Mardian enters)

Oh! thy vile lady!

She has robbed me of my sword.

Mardian: No, Mark Anthony, my mistress loved thee and her fortunes mingled with thine entirely.

Mark Anthony: Hence, saucy eunuch; peace!

She hath betrayed me and shall die the death.

Mardian: Death of one person can be paid but once, and that she has discharged.

What thou wouldst do is done unto thy hand.

The last she spake was Mark Anthony! most noble Mark Anthony! Then in the midst a tearing groan did break the name of Mark Anthony; it was divided between her heart and lips.

She rendered life, thy name so buried in her.

Mark Anthony: Dead, then?

Mardian: Dead.

Mark Anthony: Unarm, Eros; the long day's task is done,
And we must sleep.

Mark Anthony: (To Mardian)

That thou depart'st hence safe; does pay thy labour richly; go.

(Mardian exits)

Off, pluck off, the seven-fold shield of Ajax cannot keep the battery from my heart.

Oh cleave my sides! Heart once be stronger than thy continent, crack thy frail case!

Apace, Eros, apace, no more a soldier, bruised pieces; go from me a while, you have been nobly borne.

(Eros exits)

I will overtake thee, Cleopatra, and weep for my pardon.

So it must be, for now, all length is torture since the torch is out.

Lie down and stray no farther, now all labour Mars what it does; yea, the very force entangles itself with strength.

Seal then, and all is done.

Eros! I come my queen, Eros! Stay for me.

Where souls do couch on flowers, we'll hand in hand, and with our sprightly port make the ghosts gaze.

Dido and her Aeneas shall want troops, and all the haunt be ours.

Come, Eros, Eros!

(Eros re-enters)

Eros: What would my lord?

Mark Anthony: Since Cleopatra died, I have lived in such dishonour that the gods
detest my baseness.

Mark Anthony: I, that with my sword quarter'd the world and over green Neptune's back with ships made cities, condemn myself to lack the courage of a woman; less noble mind than she, which by her death our Caesar now claims he is conqueror of himself.

Thou art sworn, Eros, that when the exigent should come, which now is come indeed, when I should see behind me the inevitable prosecution of disgrace and horror; that on my command thou then wouldst kill me.

Do it, the time is come, thou strikest not me, it is Caesar thou defeat'st; put colour in thy cheek.

Eros: The gods withhold me!

Shall I do that which all the Parthian darts, though enemy, lost aim and could not?

Mark Anthony: Eros, wouldst thou be windowed in great Rome and see thy master thus with pleached arms, bending down his corrigible neck, his face subdued to penetrative shame; whilst the wheeled seat of fortunate Caesar drawn before him, branded his baseness that ensued?

Eros: I would not see it.

Mark Anthony: Come, then; for with a wound I must be cured. Draw that thy honest sword, which thou hast worn, most useful for thy country.

Eros: Oh, sir, pardon me!

Mark Anthony: When I did make thee free, sworest thou not then to do this when I bade thee?

Do it at once, or thy precedent services are all but accidents unpurposed.

Draw, and come.

Eros: Turn from me, then, that noble countenance, wherein the worship of the whole world lies.

Mark Anthony: Lords thee!

(Turning from him)

Eros: My sword is drawn.

Mark Anthony: Then let it do at once the thing why thou hast drawn it.

Eros: My dear master, my captain, and my emperor; let me say, before I strike this bloody stroke, farewell.

Mark Anthony: it is said, man; and farewell.

Eros: Farewell, great chief. Shall I strike now?

Mark Anthony: Now, Eros.

Eros: Why, there then, thus I do escape the sorrow of Mark Anthony's death.

(Kills himself)

Mark Anthony: Thrice-nobler than myself!

Thou teachest me, Oh valiant Eros, what I should, and thou couldst not.

My queen and Eros have by their brave instruction got upon me a nobleness in record; but I will be a bridegroom in my death, and run into it as to a lover's bed.

Come then, and Eros, thy master dies thy scholar; to do thus.

(Falling on his sword)

I learned of thee.

How! not dead? not dead?

The guard, oh! Oh, dispatch me!

(Enter Dercetas and Guard)

First Guard: What's the noise?

Mark Anthony: I have done my work in, friends, oh make an end of what I have begun.

Second Guard: The star is fallen.

First Guard: And time is at his period.

All: Alas, and woe!

Mark Anthony: Let him that loves me strike me dead.

First Guard: Not I.

Second Guard: Nor I.

Third Guard: Nor any one.

(Exit Guard)

Dercetas: Thy death and fortunes bid thy followers fly. This sword but shown to Caesar, with this tidings, shall enter me with him.

(Diomedes enters)

Diomedes: Where's Mark Anthony?

Dercetas: There, Diomedes there.

Diomedes: Lives he?

Wilt thou not answer, man?

(Exit Dercetas)

Mark Anthony: Art thou there, Diomedes? Draw thy sword, and give me sufficing strokes for death.

Diomedes: Most absolute lord, my mistress Cleopatra sent me to thee.

Mark Anthony: When did she send thee?

Diomedes: Now, my lord.

Mark Anthony: Where is she?

Diomedes: Locked in her monument. She had a prophesying fear of what hath come to pass, for when she saw which never shall be found, you did suspect she had disposed with Caesar, and that your rage would not be purged; she sent you word she was dead. but, fearing since how it might work, hath sent me to proclaim the truth, and I am come,

I dread, too late.

Mark Anthony: Too late, good Diomedes. call my guard, I prithee.

Diomedes: What, oh the emperor's guard! The guard, what oh! Come, your lord calls!

(Enter four or five of the Guard of Mark Anthony)

Mark Anthony: Bear me, good friends, where Cleopatra bides, it is the last service that I shall command you.

First Guard: Woe, woe are we, sir, you may not live to wear, all your true followers out.

All: Most heavy day!

Mark Anthony: Nay, good my fellows, do not please sharp fate to grace it with your sorrows.

Bid that welcome which comes to punish us, and we punish it seeming to bear it lightly.

Take me up, I have led you soft, carry me now, good friends, and have my thanks for

(Exit, bearing Mark Anthony)

Act IV, Scene 15

The same general location. A monument.

(Cleopatra enters and her maids aloft, with Charmain and Iras)

Cleopatra: Oh Charmain, I will never go from hence.

Charmain: Be comforted, dear madam.

Cleopatra: No, I will not, all strange and terrible events are welcome; but comforts we despise our size of sorrow' proportioned to our cause must be as great as that which makes it.

(Diomedes enters)

How now! Is he dead?

Diomedes: His death's upon him, but not dead.

Look out of the other side your monument; his guard have brought him thither.

(Enter, below, Mark Anthony, borne by the Guard)

Cleopatra: Oh sun, burn the great sphere thou movest in! Darkling stand

The varying shore of the world.

Oh Mark Anthony, Mark Anthony, Mark Anthony!

Help, Charmain, help, Iras, help; help, friends, let's draw him hither.

Mark Anthony: Peace!

Not Caesar's valour hath overthrown Mark Anthony, but Mark Anthony's hath triumphed on itself.

Cleopatra: So it should be, that none but Mark Anthony should conquer Mark Anthony; but woe it is so!

Mark Anthony: I am dying, Egypt, dying; only I here importune death awhile, until of many thousand kisses the poor last

I lay up thy lips.

Cleopatra: I dare not, dear, dear my lord, pardon, I dare not. Lest I be taken, not the imperious show, of the full-fortuned Caesar ever shall be rebirthed with me; if knife, drugs, serpents, have edge, sting, or operation; I am safe.

Your wife Octavia, with her modest eyes and still conclusion shall acquire no honour demuring upon me. But come, come, Mark Anthony, help me, my women,

We must draw thee up, assist, good friends.

Mark Anthony: Oh, quick, or I am gone.

Cleopatra: Here's sport indeed! How heavy weighs my lord! Our strength is all gone into heaviness that makes the weight. Had I great Juno's power, the strong-winged Mercury should fetch thee up, and set thee by Jupiter's side.

Yet come a little wishes, were ever fools, Oh, come, come, come.

(They heave Mark Anthony aloft to Cleopatra)

And welcome, welcome! Die where thou hast lived.

Quicken with kissing, had my lips that power, thus would I wear them out.

All: A heavy sight!

Mark Anthony: I am dying, Egypt dying, give me some wine, and let me speak a little.

Cleopatra: No, let me speak, and let me rail so high that the false housewife fortune break her wheel; provoked by my offence.

Mark Anthony: One word, sweet queen.

If Caesar seek your honour, with your safety. Oh!

Cleopatra: They do not go together.

Mark Anthony: Gentle, hear me.

None about Caesar trust but Proculeius.

Cleopatra: My resolution and my hands I'll trust none about Caesar.

Mark Anthony: The miserable change now at my end

Lament nor sorrow at, but please your thoughts in feeding them with those my former fortunes wherein I lived, the greatest prince of the world, the noblest; and do now not basely die.

Not cowardly put off my helmet to my countryman, a Roman by a Roman

Valiantly vanquished.

Now my spirit is going, I can no more.

Cleopatra: Noblest of men, woo it die?

Hast thou no care of me? shall I abide In this dull world, which in thy absence is

no better than a sty?

Oh, see, my women,

(Mark Anthony dies)

Cleopatra: The crown oh the earth doth melt. My lord!

Oh, withered is the garland of the war, the soldier's pole is fallen.

Young boys and girls are level now with men, the odds is gone, and there is nothing left remarkable beneath the visiting moon.

(Faints)

Charmain: Oh, quietness, lady!

Iras: She is dead too, our sovereign.

Charmain: Lady!

Iras: Madam!

Charmain: Oh madam, madam, madam!

Iras: Royal Egypt, Empress!

Charmain: Peace, peace, Iras!

Cleopatra: No more, but even a woman, and commanded by such poor passion as the maid that milks and does the meanest chores.

It were for me to throw my sceptre at the injurious gods, to tell them that this world did equal theirs till they had stollen our jewel.

All's but naught; patience is scottish, and impatience does become a dog that's mad; then is it sin to rush into the secret house of death were death dare come to us?

How do you, women?

What, what! good cheer! Why, how now, Charmain!

My noble girls! Ah, women, women, look, our lamp is spent, it's out! Good sirs, take heart, we'll bury him; and then, what's brave, what's noble,

Let's do it after the high Roman fashion, and make death proud to take us.\

Come away, this case of that huge spirit now is cold.

Ah, women, women! Come; we have no friend but resolution, and the briefest end.

(Exit; those above bearing off Mark Anthony's body)

Act V, Scene 1

Alexandria. Octavius Caesar's camp.

(Octavius Caesar, Agrippa, Dolabella, Mecaena, Gallus, Proculeius, and others, his council of war enter)

Octavius: Go to him, Dolabella, bid him yield, being so frustrate; tell him he mocks the pauses that he makes.

Dolabella: Caesar, I shall:

(Exit)

(Dercetas enters with the sword of Mark Anthony)

Octavius: Wherefore is that? and what art thou that darest appear thus to us?

Dercetas: I am called Dercetas; Mark Anthony I served who best was worthy, best to be served whilst he stood up and spoke. He was my master and I wore my life to spend upon his haters.

If thou please to take me to thee, as I was to him I'll be to Caesar; if thou pleasest not, I yield thee up my life.

Octavius: What is it thou say'st?

Dercetas: I say, Oh Caesar, Mark Anthony is dead.

Octavius: The breaking of so great a thing should make a greater crack; the round world should have shook lions into civil streets, and citizens to their dens.

The death of Mark Anthony is not a single doom, in the name lay a moiety of the world.

Dercetas: He is dead, Caesar, not by a public minister of justice, nor by a hired knife; but that self hand; which writ his honour in the acts it did hath.

With the courage which the heart did lend, it splitted the heart; this is his sword, I robbed his wound of it, behold it stained with his most noble blood.

Octavius: Look you sad, friends? The gods rebuke me, but it is tidings to wash the eyes of kings.

Agrippa: And strange it is, that nature must compel us to lament our most persisted deeds.

Mecaenas: His taints and honours waged equal with him.

Agrippa: A rarer spirit never did steer humanity, but you, gods, whose will give us some faults to make us men.

Caesar is touched.

Mecaenas: When such a spacious mirror's set before him, he needs must see himself.

Octavius: Oh Mark Anthony!

I have followed thee to this; but we do lance diseases in our bodies.

Octavius: I must perforce, have shown to thee such a declining day, or look on thine we could not stall together in the whole world; but yet let me lament, with tears as sovereign as the blood of hearts. That thou, my brother, my competitor; in top of all design my mate in empire.

Friend and companion in the front of war, the arm of mine own body, and the heart where mine his thoughts did kindle, that our stars, as unreconciliable, should divide our equalness to this.

Hear me, good friends, but I will tell you at some greeter season.

(Enter an Egyptian)

The business of this man looks out of him, we'll hear him what he says.

Whence are you?

Egyptian: A poor Egyptian, yet, the queen my mistress, confined in all she has, her monument, of thy intents desires instruction.

That she preparedly may frame herself to the way she's forced to.

Octavius: Bid her have good heart, she soon shall know of us, by some of ours; how honourable and how kindly we determine for her, for Caesar cannot live to be ungentle.

Egyptian: So the gods preserve thee!

(Exit)

Octavius: Come hither, Proculeius.

Go and say, we purpose her no shame, give her what comforts the quality of her passion shall require; lest in her greatness, by some mortal stroke she do defeat us.

For her life in Rome would be eternal in our triumph go and with your speediest bring us what she says, and how you find of her.

Proculeius: Caesar, I shall:

(Exit)

Octavius: Gallus, go you along.

(Exit Gallus)

Where's Dolabella

To second Proculeius?

All: Dolabella!

Octavius: Let him alone, for I remember now how he's employed; he shall in time be ready.

Go with me to my tent, where you shall see how hardly I was drawn into this war, how calm and gentle I proceeded still in all my writings.

Go with me, and see what I can show in this.

(Exit)

Act V, Scene 2

A room in the monument. (Alexandria)

(Cleopatra, Charmain, and Iras enter)

Cleopatra: My desolation does begin to make a better life, it is paltry to be Caesar; not being Fortune.

He's but Fortune's knave, a minister of her will: and it is great to do that thing that ends all other deeds; which shackles accidents and bolts up change, which sleeps, and never palates more the dug, the beggar's nurse and Caesar's.

(Proculeius, Gallus, Soldiers enters the gates of the monument)

Proculeius: Caesar sends greeting to the Queen of Egypt, and bids thee study on what fair demands thou mean'st to have him grant thee.

Cleopatra: What's thy name?

Proculeius: My name is Proculeius:

Cleopatra: Mark Anthony did tell me of you, bade me trust you; but I do not greatly care to be deceived; that I have no use for trusting. If your master would have a queen his beggar, you must tell him that, majesty, to keep decorum, must no less beg than a kingdom; if he please to give me conquered Egypt for my son,

He gives me so much of mine own, as I will kneel to him with thanks.

Proculeius: Be of good cheer; you're fallen into a princely hand, fear nothing, make your full reference freely to my lord, who is so full of grace that it flows over on all that need.

Let me report to him your sweet dependency, and you shall find a conqueror that will pray in aid for kindness; where he for grace is kneeled to.

Cleopatra: Pray you, tell him I am his fortune's vassal, and I send him the greatness he has got.

I hourly learn a doctrine of obedience, and would gladly look him in the face.

Proculeius: This I'll report, dear lady, have comfort, for I know your plight is pitied of him that caused it.

Gallus: You see how easily she may be surprised:

(Here Proculeius and two of the Guard ascend the monument by a ladder placed against a window, and having descended come behind Cleopatra. Some of the Guard unbar and open the gates)

(To Proculeius and the Guard)

Guard her till Caesar come.

(Exit)

Iras: Royal queen!

Charmain: Oh Cleopatra! Thou art taken, queen.

Cleopatra: Quick, quick, good hands.

(Drawing a dagger)

Proculeius: Hold, worthy lady, hold.

(Seizes and disarms her)

Do not yourself such wrong, who are in this relieved but not betrayed.

Cleopatra: What, of death too, that rids our dogs of languish?

Proculeius: Cleopatra, do not abuse my master's bounty by the undoing of yourself; let the world see his nobleness well acted, which your death will never let come forth.

Cleopatra: Where art thou, death?

Come hither, come! come, come, and take a queen worthy many babes and beggars!

Proculeius: Oh, temperance, lady!

Cleopatra: Sir, I will eat no meat, I'll not drink, sir; If idle talk will once be necessary, I'll not sleep neither.

This mortal house I'll ruin, do Caesar what he can; know sir, that I will not wait opinion at your master's court; nor once be chastised with the sober eye of dull Octavia.

Shall they hoist me up and show me to the shouting varletry of censuring Rome?

Rather a ditch in Egypt be gentle grave unto me! Rather on Niles' mud, lay me stark naked, and let the water-flies blow me into abhorring!

Rather make my country's high pyramides my gibbet, and hang me up in chains!

Proculeius: You do extend

These thoughts of horror further than you shall find cause in Caesar.

(Enter Dolabella)

Dolabella: Proculeius,

What thou hast done thy master Caesar knows, and he hath sent for thee.

Dolabella: For the queen, I'll take her to my Guard.

Proculeius: So, Dolabella, it shall content me best, be gentle to her.

(To Cleopatra)

To Caesar I will speak what you shall please, if you'll employ me to him.

Cleopatra: Say, I would die.

(Exit Proculeius and Soldiers)

Dolabella: Most noble empress, you have heard of me?

Cleopatra: I cannot tell.

Dolabella: Assuredly you know me.

Cleopatra: No matter, sir, what I have heard or known, you laugh when boys or women tell their dreams; is it not your trick?

Dolabella: I understand not, madam.

Cleopatra: I dreamed there was an Emperor Mark Anthony. Oh, such another sleep, that I might see but such another man!

Dolabella: If it might please ye.

Cleopatra: His face was as the heavens; and therein stuck a sun and moon which kept their course; and lighted the earth.

Dolabella: Most sovereign creature.

Cleopatra: His legs bestrid the ocean, his reared arm crested the world.

His voice was propertied as all the tuned spheres, and that to friends, but when he meant to quail and shake the orb he was as rattling thunder; for his bounty there was no winter in it.

An autumn it was, that grew the more by reaping his delights, were dolphin-like; they showed his back above the element they lived in. In his livery walked crowns and crownets, realms and islands were as plates dropped from his pocket.

Dolabella: Cleopatra!

Cleopatra: Think you there was, or might be, such a man as this I dreamed of?

Dolabella: Gentle madam, no.

Cleopatra: You lie, up to the hearing of the gods, but if there be, or ever were one such.

It's past the size of dreaming, nature wants stuff to live strange forms with fancy; yet to imagine, and Mark Anthony were nature's piece against fancy, condemning shadows quite.

Dolabella: Hear me, good madam.

Your loss is as yourself, great; and you bear it as answering to the weight would.

I might never overtake pursued success, but I do feel, by the rebound of yours, a grief that smites my very heart at root.

Cleopatra: I thank you, sir; know you what Caesar means to do with me?

Dolabella: I am loath to tell you what I would you knew.

Cleopatra: Nay, pray you, sir,

Dolabella: Though he be honourable.

Cleopatra: He'll lead me, then, in triumph?

Dolabella: Madam, he will, I know itt.

(Flourish delivered, and shouts within area, "Make way there for Octavius Caesar!")

(Octavius Caesar, Gallus, and Proculeius Mecaenas, Seleucus and entourage enter)

Octavius: Which is the Queen of Egypt?

Dolabella: It is the emperor, madam.

(Cleopatra kneels)

Octavius: Arise, you shall not kneel.

I pray you, rise, rise, Egypt.

Cleopatra: Sir, the gods

Will have it thus my master and my lord, I must obey.

Octavius: Take to you no hard thoughts.

The record of what injuries you did us, though written in our flesh we shall remember as things but done by chance.

Cleopatra: Sole sir of the world, I cannot project mine own cause so well to make it clear; but do confess I have been laden with like frailties which before have often shamed our sex.

Octavius: Cleopatra, know, we will extenuate rather than enforce, if you apply yourself to our intents; which towards you are most gentle you shall find a benefit in this change; but if you seek to lay on me a cruelty, by taking Mark Anthony's course, you shall bereave yourself of my good purposes, and put your children to that destruction which I'll guard them from.

If thereon you rely. I'll take my leave.

Cleopatra: And may, through all the world it is yours, and we, your scutcheons; and your signs of conquest shall hang in what place you please.

Here, my good lord.

Octavius: You shall advise me in all for Cleopatra.

Cleopatra: This is the brief of money, plate, and jewels, I am possessed of, it is exactly valued; not petty things admitted.

Where's Seleucus?

Seleucus: Here, madam.

Cleopatra: This is my treasurer let him speak, my lord, upon his peril; that I have reserved to myself nothing.

Speak the truth, Seleucus.

Seleucus: Madam, I had rather seal my lips, than to my peril, speak that which is not.

Cleopatra: What have I kept back?

Seleucus: Enough to purchase what you have made known.

Octavius: Nay, blush not Cleopatra; I approve your wisdom in the deed.

Cleopatra: See, Caesar! Oh behold, how pomp is followed! Mine will now be yours, and should we shift estates yours would be mine. The ingratitude of this Seleucus does even make me wild, Oh slave of no more trust than love that's hired!

What, goest thou back? thou shalt go back, I warrant thee; but I'll catch thine eyes, though they had wings.

Slave, soulless villain, dog!

Oh rarely base!

Octavius: Good queen, let us entreat you.

Cleopatra: Oh Caesar, what a wounding shame is this.

That thou, vouchsafing here to visit me; doing the honour of thy lordliness.

To one so meek that mine own servant should parcel the sum of my disgraces by

addition of his envy!

Say, good Caesar, that I some lady trifles have reserved, immoment toys, things of such dignity as we greet modern friends withal; and say; some nobler token I have kept apart for Livia and Octavia to induce their mediation.

Must I be unfolded with one that I have no desires to? The gods! It smites me beneath the fall I have.

(To Seleucus)

Prithee, go hence.

Or I shall show the cinders of my spirits through the ashes of my chance: wert thou a man,

Thou wouldst have mercy on me.

Octavius: Foirbear.

(Seleucus exits)

Cleopatra: Be it known, that we, the greatest, are misthought for things that others do. and, when we fall we answer others' merits in our name; are therefore to be pitied.

Octavius: Cleopatra, not what you have reserved, nor what acknowledged, put we in the roll of conquest; still be it yours, bestow it at your pleasure and believe Caesar's no merchant to make prize with you, of things that merchants sold.

Therefore be cheered, make not your thoughts your prisons, no dear queen for we intend so to dispose you as yourself shall give us counsel.

Feed, and sleep, our care and pity is so much upon you; that we remain your friend and so, adieu.

Cleopatra: My master, and my lord!

Octavius: Not so. Adieu.

(Flourishing delivered. Exit Octavius Caesar and his entourage)

Cleopatra: He words me, girls, he words me, that I should not be noble to myself; but, hark thee, Charmain.

(Whispers Charmain)

Iras: Finish, good lady; the bright day is done, and we are for the dark.

Cleopatra: Hail thee again, I have spoke already and it is provided; go put it to the haste.

Charmain: Madam, I will.

(Dolabella re-enters)

Dolabella: Where is the queen?

Charmain: Behold, sir.

(Exit)

Cleopatra: Dolabella!

Dolabella: Madam, as thereto sworn by your command, which my love makes religion to obey; I tell you this, Caesar through Syria intends his journey, and within three days you with your children will he send before.

Make your best use of this, I have performed your pleasure and my promise.

Cleopatra: Dolabella, I shall remain your debtor.

Dolabella: I your servant, adieu good queen, I must attend on Caesar.

Cleopatra: Farewell, and thanks.

(Dolabella Exits)

Now, Iras, what think'st thou?

Thou, an Egyptian puppet, shalt be shown in Rome, as well as I; mechanic slaves with greasy aprons, rules, and hammers, shall uplift us to the view, in their thick breaths, rank of gross diet, shall be enclouded, and forced to drink their vapour.

Iras: The gods forbid!

Cleopatra: Nay, it is most certain, Iras, saucy lictors will catch at us like strumpets and scald rhymers; ballad us out on tune.

The quick comedians, extemporally, will stage us and present our Alexandrian revels Mark Anthony; we Shall be brought drunken forth, and I shall see some squeaking Cleopatra boy my greatness In the posture of a whore.

Iras: Oh the good gods!

Cleopatra: Nay, that's certain.

Iras: I'll never see t; for, I am sure, my nails are stronger than mine eyes.

Cleopatra: Why, that's the way to fool their preparation, and to conquer their most absurd intents.

(Charmain re-enters)

Cleopatra: Now, Charmain! Show me my women, like a queen, go fetch my best attires.

I am again for Cydnus, to meet Mark Anthony, sirrah Iras, go now noble Charmain; we'll dispatch indeed And when thou hast done this chore, I'll give thee leave To play till doomsday.

Bring our crown and All.

Wherefore's this noise?

(Exit Iras while there is a noise within)

(Enter a Guardsman)

Guard: Here is a rural fellow that will not be denied, your highness, presence; he brings you figs.

Cleopatra: Let him come in.

(Exit Guardsman)

What poor an instrument may do a noble deed! He brings me liberty. My resolution's placed, and I have nothing of woman in me; now from head to foot I am marble-constant, now of the fleeting moon, no planet is of mine.

(Guardsman re-enters with Jester bringing in a basket)

Guard: This is the man.

Cleopatra: Avoid, and leave him.

(Exit Guardsman)

Hast thou the pretty worm of Nilus there, that kills and pains not?

Jester: Truly I have him, but I would not be the party that should desire you to touch him, for his biting is immortal; those that do die of it do seldom or never recover.

Cleopatra: Rememberest thou any that have died on it?

Jester: Very many, men and women too.
I heard of one of them no longer than yesterday, a very honest woman, but something given to lie; as a woman should not do, but in the way of honesty.
How she died of the biting of it, what pain she felt, truly she makes a very good report of the worm; but he that will believe all that they say shall never be saved by half that they do.
But this is most fallible, the worm's an odd worm.

Cleopatra: Get thee hence, farewell.

Jester: I wish you all joy of the worm.

(Setting down his basket)

Cleopatra: Farewell.

Jester: You must think this, look you, that the worm will do his kind.

Cleopatra: Ay, ay; farewell.

Jester: Look you, the worm is not to be trusted, but in the keeping of wise people for, indeed there is no goodness in worm.

Cleopatra: Take thou no care, it shall be heeded.
Jester: Very good.
Give it nothing, I pray you, for it is not worth the feeding.
Cleopatra: Will it eat me?
Jester: You must not think I am so simple but I know the devil himself will not eat a woman.
I know that a woman is a dish for the gods, if the devil dress her not; but truly, these same whoreson devils do the gods great harm in their women, for in every ten that they make, the devils mar five.
Cleopatra: Well, get thee gone, farewell.
Jester: Yes, forsooth: I wish you joy of the worm.
(Exit)
(Iras re-enters with a robe, crown)
Cleopatra: Give me my robe, put on my crown; I have immortal longings in me, now no more.
The juice of Egypt's grape shall moist this lip, yare, yare, good Iras; quick.
Methinks I hear Mark Anthony call, I see him rouse himself to praise my noble act; I hear him mock; the luck of Caesar, which the gods give men to excuse their after wrath.
Husband I come now to that name my courage prove my title!
I am fire and air, my other elements I give to baser life.
So have you done? Come then, and take the last warmth of my lips.
Farewell, kind Charmain, Iras, long farewell.
(Kisses them. Iras falls and dies)

Have I the aspic in my lips? Dost fall?

If thou and nature can so gently part, the stroke of death is as a lover's pinch; which hurts, and is desired.

Dost thou lie still? If thus thou vanishest, thou tell'st the world it is not worth leave-taking.

Charmain: Dissolve, thick cloud, and rain; that I may say, the gods themselves do weep!

Cleopatra: This proves me base if she first meet the curled Mark Anthony, he'll make demand of her, and spend that kiss; which is my heaven to have.

Come, thou mortal wretch.

(To an asp, which she applies to her breast)

With thy sharp teeth this knot intrinsicate of life at once untie, poor venomous fool ,

be angry and dispatch.

Oh, couldst thou speak, that I might hear thee call great Caesar ass unpolicied!

Charmain: Oh eastern star!

Cleopatra: Peace, peace!

Dost thou not see my baby at my breast, that sucks the nurse asleep?

Charmain: Oh, break! Oh, break!

Cleopatra: As sweet as balm, as soft as air, as gentle, Oh Mark Anthony!

Nay, I will take thee too.

(Applying another asp to her arm)

What should I stay.

(Dies)

Charmain: In this vile world? So, fare thee well.

Now boast thee, death, in thy possession lies a woman unparalleled. Downy windows close, and golden Phoebus never beheld of eyes again so royal!

Your crown's awry, I'll mend it, and then play.

(Guard rushes in)

First Guard: Where is the queen?

Charmain: Speak softly, wake her not.

First Guard: Caesar hath sent.

Charmain: Too slow a Messenger.

(Applies an asp)

Oh, come apace, dispatch! I partly feel thee.

First Guard: Approach, oh! All's not well, Caesar's beguiled.

Second Guard: There's Dolabella sent from Caesar; call him.

First Guard: What work is here! Charmain, is this well done?

Charmain: It is well done, and fitting for a princess descended of so many royal kings.

Ah, soldier!

(Dies)

(Dolabella re-enters)

Dolabella: How goes it here?

Second Guard: All dead.

Dolabella: Caesar, thy thoughts touch their effects in this, thyself art coming to see performed the dreaded act which thou so sought'st to hinder.

(Within 'A way there, a way for Caesar!')

(Re-enter Octavius Caesar and all his entourage marching)

Dolabella: Oh sir, you are too sure an augurer, that you did fear is done.

Octavius: Bravest at the last, she levelled at our purposes, and being royal took her own way.

The manner of their deaths? I do not see them bleed.

Dolabella: Who was last with them?

First Guard: A simple countryman, that brought her figs, this was his basket.

Octavius: Poisoned, then.

First Guard: Oh Caesar, this Charmain lived but now, she stood and spake; I found her trimming up the diadem on her dead mistress, tremblingly she stood and on the sudden dropped.

Octavius: Oh noble weakness! If they had swallowed poison, it would appear by external swelling; but she looks like sleep, as she would catch another Mark Anthony in her strong toil of grace.

Dolabella: Here, on her breast, there is a vent of blood and something blown, the like is on her arm.

First Guard: This is an aspic's trail, and these fig-leaves have slime upon them, such as the aspic leaves upon the caves of Nile.

Octavius: Most probable that so she died, for her physician tells me she hath pursued conclusions infinite of easy ways to die.

Take up her bed and bear her women from the monument.

Octavius: She shall be buried by her Mark Anthony, no grave upon the earth shall clip in it a pair so famous.

High events as these strike those that make them; and their story is no less in pity than his glory which brought them to be lamented.

Our army shall in solemn show attend this funeral, and then to Rome.

Come Dolabella, see high order in this great solemnity.

(Exit)

The End

Description of Titles

The Comedy of Errors
Caught in a land of embittered woman and war, caught in months of strife, where a merchant's visit offers little natural relief. The fleeting moment of approving gold, inspire further bitterness, upon an approach to the marketplace, and then the women that occupy within them.

19 Characters

The Taming of the Shrew
Arrangements are made to spencer would be suiters to melt the splendors of a strong willed women. The winning is found pledged, influencing maids to seek their turns, and meanwhile terms required, an authentic spirit that they will/would wed soon.

34 Characters

Love's Labor's Lost
The house of a scholarly pursuit, returns into an expressive, either poetic or drunken as highlighting the gold-slur filled house of charms and dance like rhymes

19 Characters

A Midsummer Night's Dream
Journey into a land of fairies, where creatures are found to have the same issues as nobilities. Exemplifying, perhaps, there's no place like home. Meet fairies as they frolic and play the noble hearts and sway, posed in the recesses of night, and mystic lands of a faraway kingdom.

22 Characters

The Merchant of Venice

An angry Shylock brings to trial a merchant, over a lover's quarrel disrupted, demanding pounds of flesh. With no desires for even three times the amount, the Shylock demands his vengeance at heart.

22 Characters

The Merry Wives of Windsor
Mistresses and lords try and relate towards one another, as various important community figures come to have their word/seek the hostesses. Pleasantries are exchanged as a range of charms are expressed, until conversation resembled so to folly.

23 Characters

Much Ado About Nothing
Soldiery level consideration occupy the gossip, as several hostilities are summoned up, onto heart related matter. Also in conflict. The latter portion of the story lightens up to a women's home and pleasantries. Thereafter, a general search and care in actions, creating response phrasing poetic to the responses of leadership parading, until an end full of sensitivity asking gently questions, onto kisses

23 Characters

As You Like It
Troubled lower nobles venture about daily business, with some mild graces towards the ladies found. In need of relief or play, the Duke and family members take to the woods, where jests of drinking turn into troubled amusements, or warmth of a women's heart.

26 Characters

Troilus and Cressida

The infamous Greek battle for Troy. A large army arrives to take back the lost love of a humiliated foe. Both sides mobilize heroes onto the field, as soldiers and generals move to the side, and let strategies and fate take their course.

21+ Characters

All's Well That Ends Well

A tale of delightful, womanly gossip of a prestigious sort, until the French King has his word on the excellence of others. The story initially revolves around a strong willed countess, whose courteous pose and insight, reflect a nobility reflective of the house and court (council). Dialogue therein revolving around the councils rather, to exemplify (court counselling women).

25 Characters

Measure for Measure

Statesmen discourse leading with time to a personal reflection. Strolling Dukes and strong willed women occupy the background, where high-function status and family discourse intertwine within formalities (of administrative foresight, expression) observed.

24 Characters

Richard III

An in palace drama with King Richard the 3rd, Queen Elizabeth, and Queen Margret. Onto a haunting reunion, as the state processes royal executions.

61+ Characters

The Life and Death of King John
King John and Queen Elinor entertain the royal court, where a bastard has come to make his day. Strategic deployments of influence are exemplified, as the bastard plots about until alerts, alarm corruption has delivered trouble makers known.

24 Characters

Romeo and Juliet
Lovers emerge within a city gripped with two feuding houses apposed. As turmoil are caught in bitter heat, the lover's. Bliss and undying pledge becomes them, onto the eternal soul (of love and romance).

33 Characters

Othello
A hopeful Othello calls upon the favor of allies based on proposed merits, which called upon allies and foes to him. In a mixed response, allies and foes campaign both against Othello, becoming a bitter, personal tangle over a mislead love adventure representing the future of either fates

25 Characters

Macbeth
A desperate Macbeth ventures towards witches to tell fortune, returning to a castle haunted by ghost/old-spirits. Macbeth's worries become frightful nightmares, along the despair of the household around him.

39 Characters

Mark Antony and Cleopatra
The relations or affections of Mark Anthony and Cleopatra, onto the strategic interactions between Mark Anthony and Octavius. The discourse moves to the Octavius house, revealing Octavia, and later then, Pompey in the background. Overall the focus retains upon Mark Anthony, Cleopatra, and Octavius.

56+ Characters

Coriolanus
Citizens riot during a famine, while the state administrative intervenes and otherwise discourses the seriousness of the matter and war. Lady's calm the general ambience, until the sword is mobilized to defend the gates, , while the plight of people is nevertheless heard convincing Roman elites the problem is being found/fought within.

60 Characters

Pericles Prince of Tyre
A thoughtful/reflective Pericles interposes his good will and well-meaning nature, which leads him to visit fishermen friends, and onto state function. Pericles is then confronted, required to (take a plunge) to marry, embedding him deeper into ocean stock of sea life among sailors experience and merchant owners, investing his interest as babe, securing his destiny as then, future king

44 Characters

Cymbeline
Cymbeline, friend or loyalist to the first Caesars, is summoned into battle. Meanwhile there are personal matters to attend to within the noble house.

41 Characters

The Winter's Tale
A gossipy tale of high office, administrative daily insight onto the tender meaning of things and people an how they unite unwittingly at the discourse of their respected hierarchies of partnership. Profoundness therein inspiring the recounts of clown and child, as examples perhaps of what state administration and or nobility's company keeps.

34+ Characters

The Tempest
After an earth shattering storm, a fairy dwelling world is found. There magic and graces are there in song, glory and praises.

21 Characters

The Two Gentlemen of Verona
Loving beginnings, yet far too. General virtues going upwards in hierarchies, with overall chivalrous wits.

Twelfth Night
An evening in the company of sound gatherings, seemingly a docile manner recount version of noble delights. In similarities of the pose, composing an environment of insight and oversight.

Henry the 8th
Across chamber and palace, Dukes and lords, until Queen Katharine's and King Henry VIII's present their graces, conversing the Cardinal then. The signs then, an Elizabeth is born.

Richard II
King Richard the 2nd readies the armed forces at the sound of alarm, while later Henry IV is near for discussion. King Richard the 2nd and his groom.

Henry V
King Henry the 5th, as found across his palace, until a readiness for war. King Henry the 5th and the French King, with armies both have at it.

Henry VI, Part 1
Funeral of King Henry the 5th, Henry VI makes his approach to France. Henry VI fashions as thy lord protector.

Henry VI, Part 2
King Henry the 6th, where the Cardinal is seen mocking protectors with praise, as all the rage. Queen Margaret at King Henry VI, until the end.

Henry VI, Part 3
King Henry VI is busy fighting a succession of battles, France and England as having at it, yet again.

King Henry the 5th
King Henry 5 fight his way toward France, they reach the peaceful and loving responses of a French King.

Henry IV, Part 1
King Henry the 4th, from Palace to Pub, onto the battle fields again. Until there is no rebellion.

Henry IV, Part 2
Henry IV, from Palace, Priest and then tavern, he nevertheless finds some peace, after reflection. King Henry IV, and then King Henry V as fashionable by the end.

Titus Andronicus
A story of Romans and Goths, where roman sways give way. And then to see about Goths and proving worthiness.

28 Characters

Julius Caesar
Near the Final days of the 1st Caesar, and the continuation everlasting as through Octavius.

Hamlet
Hamlet, and his father the King, the father yet a Ghost. Hamlet, not so eager to join.

King Lear
King Lear, from palace to castle, to fighting the French in the field. After battle King Lear is in bed, the Doctor discourses, what lays then now, will have an impact upon the end.

Timon of Athens
A story set in Greece, a place of poets and cultured, good graces. From Arts and daily expressive, to political and charmed.

www.ingramcontent.com/pod-product-compliance
Lightning Source LLC
Chambersburg PA
CBHW051435290426
44109CB00016B/1566